Changing

The

Spiritual Atmosphere

Kenny & Faye,

Lots of love always.

Marilyn .x

(PS 139.)

Marilyn Harry

Published by Life Publications www.lifepublications.org.uk
For more information on Life Publications please contact: info@lifepublications.org.uk

ISBN 978-1-907929-49-6
Cover Design by Graham Alder

Published by Life Publications
Contact: janholdaway@hotmail.co.uk
www.lifepublications.org.uk

Dedication

To Revivalist Sarah Trinder.
You lit up the room.
You made us laugh.
We loved the times we shared together
under the weight of the Holy Spirit.
A true friend and sister.

Acknowledgements

I would like to thank Nigel and Maria Phipps and all the Harvest Time team past and present. They are a truly passionate dedicated people. How can I ever thank you enough for your love and friendship over many years as we have travelled together proclaiming the Wonderful Gospel of our precious Lord Jesus.

Thank you as well Jan and David Holdaway without whom this book would never have been written. Thank you for encouraging me to tell these stories and your skill and dedication to make this book come to life.

Thanks as well to Lou Marston and Lea Shaw for their help in typing the manuscript.

Commendations

It is a great privilege and joy to write a few words about Marilyn Harry. I would like to call her the lady who said *'Yes'*. I have memories of Marilyn coming to Birkenhead and being asked to go to the most difficult area of the town to lead the pioneer of a new church there with very little support and she said *'Yes'*. Then she was invited to join the mission team to the Isle of Man, she said *'Yes'*. Then to stay and disciple the new converts again *'Yes'*. Then came the call of God for her to move into full time mission and again she said *'Yes'*.

Marilyn, regardless of the sacrifice, regardless of the opposition, regardless of the hopelessness that met the eye, always says *'Yes'* to God and His calling over her life. Not only is this book a 'good read', it also sets before us a testimony, an example of God's blessing on a life fully surrendered to Him.

Revd Paul Epton MBE, Chairman Wirral Christian Centre Trust
Founding Pastor Wirral Christian Centre Church

Some people write books from experience, others from knowledge, but Marilyn writes from both. Add to that the anointing of the Holy Spirit, and the result is a powerful woman of God and a powerful book. Don't read it unless you want to be inspired, encouraged, motivated and mobilised!

Nigel James
Elim Wales and Waleswide

It has been our joy and privilege to call Marilyn Harry our friend and partner in missions for nearly thirty years. Her clear declaration of the gospel and her winsome manner toward her audience have been used by the Holy Spirit to save and refresh the souls of many thousands over the years.

Mike and Mary Bave, Missionaries of the
International Church of the Foursquare Gospel
Pastors of Bethel Chapel, Pembroke Dock, Pembrokeshire

Marilyn not only preaches the Gospel – she lives it! She writes with passion and honesty and her love for Jesus shines through every chapter. This book will warm your heart and challenge you. Read on and be inspired.

Pastor Joy Gascoigne
Grimethorpe Pentecostal Church, Yorkshire

This book will inspire the Body of Christ to pray, worship, make declarations and proclamations, declaring the Word of the Lord and believing for a new move of the Spirit in salvations, signs and wonders as the spiritual atmosphere around us is changed.

Janice Bell, Apostolic Oversight and Former Senior Pastor
New Life Church Cardigan

Contents

Changing the Spiritual Atmosphere

Foreword

The first time I met Marilyn Harry I was impressed by her enthusiasm and sincerity. She's a lady with a heart for God and a great burden for her homeland of Wales. Born in the Rhondda Valley, Marilyn has travelled to various parts of the world as an itinerant Evangelist. During her ministry she has experienced being on the mountain tops and also down in the valley, but she has remained faithful to the call of God on her life – encouraging, training and equipping young and old to present the Good News of Jesus Christ.

Marilyn was trained as a midwife and began seeing the hand of God on her life from early on in her Christian walk. She is a Holy Spirit filled lady with a dynamic ministry who hears the voice of God and is not afraid to act upon His directions. The miraculous touch is always witnessed in her meetings. She is someone who has learned to wait…seek…adore her Lord.

Be ready as you read this book for the Holy Spirit to speak to you. He is well able to *ignite you*, becoming a channel on *fire* to proclaim the Good News of Jesus Christ, and to see a demonstration of God's power.

Marilyn shares her experiences with her usual open heart.

Enjoy!

Rev Denis Phillips
Former Elim Regional Superintendent for Wales

Changing the Spiritual Atmosphere

Introduction

I have wanted to write something about the importance of spiritual atmospheres for such a long time. I have travelled as an itinerant evangelist for more than thirty years, ministering in churches and evangelistic meetings throughout the UK and also in many overseas nations. Over the years I have noticed that many places I have visited have different atmospheres. This isn't just related to their natural atmosphere in terms of a place's scenery, climate, or the way people dress and behave, but spiritually each one, no matter if it's a village, town, city or different nation, has its own particular spiritual atmosphere that can affect – for good and for bad – how people respond to the Gospel or grow in their faith.

I'm sure we have all been in situations when we have walked into a room and while everything seems calm and peaceful on the surface you just know deep inside that the atmosphere is not good and as we would say in Britain, "you can cut the atmosphere with a knife." Although you do not see anything adverse or obvious, something has happened in that room before you entered it that caused an "uneasy" atmosphere. I'm sure there have been times as well when you have walked into a situation where there is just an overwhelming presence of God.

Many things change a spiritual atmosphere; actions (both good and bad), words, proclamations, worship, prayer, the sharing of our faith, the reading of God's Word publicly, forgiveness, repentance, renunciations, the condition and attitude of our human heart, acts of unity or disunity, acts of kindness, love and appreciation, to mention just a few. And of course the name of Jesus Christ, His blood and His Word.

With this in mind I have recorded some of the experiences I have had over the years of different spiritual atmospheres and situations I have encountered and how it is possible to bring about a change in the spiritual atmosphere and usher in the wonderful presence and power of the Lord Jesus Christ.

As you will be able to tell, this book is not written from the standpoint of a theologian or an expert, but from that of an ordinary evangelist who has had the wonderful privilege of preaching the message of Jesus Christ in many situations, large and small, throughout Britain and other nations. Although it is not a text book, hopefully you will be encouraged as you read that the name of Jesus Christ is still the breakthrough message and the name above all names, and that miracles still happen today, even in the UK in our post-modern society that is rapidly becoming a secular society.

Jesus is still the same *"...yesterday, today and forever."* He never changes!

The light shines in the darkness, and the darkness has not overcome it.

John 1:5

Changing the Spiritual Atmosphere

1

Early Beginnings

My story started many years ago when I was born into an ordinary family in the village of Trehafod in the Rhondda Valleys, South Wales. My father, Illtyd Harry, was a coalminer who worked underground for fifty years starting work at thirteen years of age in the local colliery in Cwm Beddau. He was a real gentleman with a shy and kind nature and a lovely smile. My mother, Mary Maud, was an extrovert and "a girl and a half", as we would say in the Rhondda. My brother, Anthony, who was eleven years older than me, was a hard worker and worked in the building trade.

I was born premature and was one of undiagnosed twin girls and only four pounds in weight, my sister died shortly after birth. I remember the school nurse coming to my home when I was seven years old and telling my parents that I could not see anything out of one of my eyes, I was blind in one eye until seven years of age but never knew. It was probably due to being born premature. I wore glasses until I was about fourteen years old and then amazingly my eyesight became totally clear!

My childhood was a happy one and we spent many hours playing on the mountainsides and walking the hillsides. I am so grateful that there was always a lot of love in our home, although like most families in our village, we were living on the bread line.

My mother's older sister, Gwendoline, who lived with us was a wonderful aunty. She was a single lady and the only one of five girls who never married. Their mother, my grandmother (who died before I was born), had become blind at the birth of the youngest baby daughter and Gwen had stayed at home to care for the family, taking in washing to provide her with a small income.

I left school at fifteen years of age and worked in a factory until I was old enough (sixteen years old), to take up a position as a cadet nurse in Llwynypia General Hospital, a thirty minute bus ride from our home. Alongside my training in the hospital I studied at the local technical college one day a week. Later, I went on to qualify as a State Registered Nurse and Midwife. This was by God's grace as I was not the best academically. The Lord really blessed me as a nurse and by the age of 25 I was a midwifery sister in East Glamorgan Hospital near Pontypridd. It was as a young midwife that one day I personally saw a wonderful miracle.

A Baby Comes Back To Life

I was on duty in the labour ward one day and a baby girl was born and lived for a short time then died. The baby was confirmed dead by the paediatrician and the parents were told the very sad news that their new-born baby had died and all attempts of resuscitation had failed. The distressed parents were moved into a side ward following this dreadful news and the death was recorded in the mother's case notes. The little lifeless body was covered with a sheet and we were all very sad. One and a quarter hours after the baby was confirmed dead, I went to wash the dead baby's body as I was going to take the baby to the parents for them to hold her. But when I took the sheet away and lifted her into my arms a miracle happened in front of my eyes. As I held the baby girl in my arms and sat her up she became alive and started to breathe and move. What a miracle! A case conference was held and the conclusion was an unexplainable case. She was followed up in the special baby clinic for two years and at two years old she was talking in complete sentences and was a perfectly healthy baby.

Hearing About Jesus

I first heard about Jesus when I was three years old and I remember, even at this tender age, thinking how I loved Jesus when the Sunday school teacher, Miss Annie Price, told the stories about Him. Miss Price was the Sunday School Superintendent and also the previous headmistress of the local primary school. She was a wonderful example for the Gospel. I had prayed every night since I was a small child and always had a longing to know God. I remember crying when I was ten years old and asking my father to buy me a Bible.

When I was nineteen years old, although life was good and I was happy at home, loved my job and had plenty of friends and a busy social life, I knew deep down something was missing. My best friend, Jennifer, had become a Christian whilst in university and every weekend would come home and with her Christian friends, she would tell me that I was a sinner and needed to put my trust in Jesus Christ. I told her she was very cheeky and that I was as good as those going to church, but deep down I did not need her to tell me that I was a sinner. I already knew my heart was far from God and that I needed His forgiveness. I loved my friends telling me though, and I wanted to know Him but I did not know how. My neighbours, Mr and Mrs Keogh, were committed Christians and went to the local Baptist Church, I knew they were praying for us as a family.

Around this time there was to be a large evangelistic event in the Cory Hall in Cardiff with the evangelist Eric Hutchings and his team. My friend, Jennifer, arranged for me and another friend, Eileen, to have a lift in a friend's car each night for the week. Hundreds of people attended and on the very last night Eileen and I were among many others who made their decision that night to follow the Lord. My family were a little bit religious but no one in our family knew the Lord apart from my Auntie Gwen and my Uncle Bill who was married to my mother's youngest sister.

Called to Preach

The night that I decided to follow the Lord Jesus is so real to me even today, as it brought about a radical change in my life. I even remember the date, it was November 14, 1970. A lovely lady spoke to me and went through the booklet *Journey Into Life* with me explaining about what it meant to be a Christian and how to take that step. I remember I sat there in that meeting in Cardiff thinking, and somehow knowing, that I was going to be a preacher, although at the time I was totally unchurched and had no understanding of what preaching really was. Within a few weeks I was asked to preach at the local sisterhood meeting in Siloam Church in Trehafod, the little Welsh chapel I went to as a child. The first message I preached was on John 3:16: *"For God so loved the world that He gave His only begotten son that whoever believes in Him, should not perish but have everlasting life."* And more and more I had an unquenchable desire to preach the Gospel and wherever I went I told everyone I met about Jesus.

At the age of 29 I left my job in the hospital and entered Elim Bible College in Capel, Surrey, graduating two years later and taking my first appointment as an assistant probationary minister in Birkenhead, Wirral, to Pastor Paul Epton, who was the Elim minister there.

Miracles on Mission

I loved every minute of being part of pioneering a new church in Milner Street, in the dock area of Birkenhead, which was part of my remit. I learned so much and it was also a great experience being part of the main church.

While at Birkenhead I took part in a mission on the Isle of Man which particularly stands out in my mind. Pastor Epton took a small team, of which I was part, and booked the Villa Marina on the seafront for ten days of meetings, and more than two hundred people responded to the Gospel. When Pastor Epton preached we saw many remarkable healings, including the healing of a young man with a curved spine. During a period of six weeks the man actually grew four inches and the curvature left his spine completely which was an amazement to all who knew him.

Some deaf received their hearing and a woman who was nearly blind received her sight. It was a real move of God. I stayed as part of the team on the island for an extra six weeks to help with the discipleship of the new believers and at the end of those six weeks, a hundred people attended one new church and fifty a second new church.

Opportunities like this set me on a firm footing to believe God for the future.

Changing the Spiritual Atmosphere

Atmospheres Change People and People Change Atmospheres

Marilyn Harry

Changing the Spiritual Atmosphere

2

Riots in the Street

The first time I really became aware of the power of a spiritual atmosphere was on my first evangelistic mission I held as a solo evangelist in a town in the North of England. It was a small situation and the pastors and I were young and quite inexperienced in mission work, but we were all keen to "have a go".

We prayed our hearts out and we fasted and we evangelised and the Lord did bless us, but one night as I was resting, the Lord reminded me of a scripture in Daniel 10. It records how Daniel fasted and prayed to the Lord for three full weeks but the answer didn't arrive until the twenty-fourth day. *"...Do not fear, Daniel, for from the first day that you set your heart to understand, and to humble yourself before your God, your words were heard; and I have come because of your words,"* Daniel 10:12.

Then it goes on to say that the prince of the kingdom of Persia had withstood the angel for twenty-one days but Michael, one of the chief princes, came to help him. I realised the connection between fasting, prayer and the words we speak in relation to heavenly intervention.

> *"If my people who are called by my name will humble themselves and pray and seek my face*

*and turn from their wicked ways, then I will
hear from heaven, and will forgive their sin
and heal their land."*

2 Chronicles 7:14

Fasting... Prayer... Words

This was brought home to me some time later when I went to
conduct my second tent mission in the early 1980s. It was held in
a borrowed 250 seater marquee in Ely, one of the suburbs of
Cardiff. I had been invited by one of the churches whose
members were working tirelessly in the area. I was going to
conduct the tent mission with them and so far all the planning
and preparation had been going very well.

The leaders of the church were good people with a heart for their
area and community. When I attended the final leadership
meeting in preparation for the evangelistic endeavour, we were
sitting in a room together. There were about ten of us and one
leader made an innocent remark to another leader across the
other side of the room and the leader to whom the remark was
made took offence at it. This continued and escalated throughout
the room with all sorts of comments being made. I sat in silence
and amazement. I watched and listened to what was happening
as words seemed to be twisted in the air and innocent remarks
were perceived as something offensive.

I was just about to say in good old fashioned Rhondda Valley
words, "I am not going to bring my borrowed 250 seater
marquee here!" When suddenly I had a revelation. Just one week
earlier there had been riots on the streets of Ely with the burning
of cars and much disturbance, and my revelation was that
because the church had not been as strong in prayer as it should
have been, the spirit of riot and lawlessness in the community

had come into the church, rather than the Spirit of the peace of Jesus, going out to the community. Realising this, I never made my remarks of not going ahead with the mission but suggested that we prayed and asked God to help us humble ourselves and repent of our words. The leaders were extremely gracious and we did this. The atmosphere in the room changed and so did the atmosphere surrounding the mission.

The mission went forward and we had a wonderful time with 96 people making first time commitments for Jesus Christ. Humility and prayer, thankfully, overcame in that situation in Ely and the Spirit of God was able to move saving many people. It was also a good lesson to learn about the power of an atmosphere around a meeting as well as in it.

Atmospheres Change People and People Change Atmospheres

The *Oxford English Dictionary* definition of atmosphere is: *"The pervading tone or mood of a place or situation."* This is the dictionary definition, but Scripture also gives us an insight. You may not be able to touch or see an atmosphere but it is still very real.

I believe that there are natural atmospheres and spiritual atmospheres. The spiritual atmosphere is the atmosphere around us of the unseen realm and is of a spiritual nature that changes us in how we think or feel or react. I think what we see in the natural often denotes what is going on in the spiritual. The reactions and words spoken and how they are understood and received are reflections of what is going on in the spiritual realm in that locality.

"While we do not look at the things which are seen, but at the things which are not seen. For the things which are seen are temporary, but the things which are not seen are eternal."

2 Corinthians 4:18

"For though we walk in the flesh, we do not war according to the flesh. For the weapons of our warfare are not carnal but mighty in God for pulling down strongholds, casting down arguments and every high thing that exalts itself against the knowledge of God, bringing every thought into captivity to the obedience of Christ."

2 Corinthians 10:3-5

The way an area is, and the way that people live and react in those areas, will often be an indication of what the ruling spirits are that dominate over the locality. For example, one of my first tent missions was to a very sleepy little Welsh village. Everything about it was "sleepy" and it was well known for depression and for youth suicides. There was a general complacency about everything that affected the natural. No doubt about it, in that situation and location the spiritual had affected the natural.

Atmospheres Can Be Changed

There are many things that can change the spiritual atmosphere and there are various accounts in the Bible where we see this happening.

Prison Breakthrough

A story which I love very much is about a move of God in the prison in Philippi, Acts 16:16-34. The two missionaries, Paul and Silas, got into trouble for casting a troublesome demon out of a girl (the demon had recognised them as being men of God). The demon had caused the girl to follow Paul and Silas to their place of prayer, daily calling out and shouting about the men and in the process causing disruption and commotion. Following the casting out of the demon the girl became free, but the two well-meaning missionaries were beaten up and put in the local prison by her owners who were angry that they had lost a source of income from the girl's psychic fortune-telling powers.

Amazingly, however, when the men ended up in the local prison a wonderful miracle happened as they prayed and sang hymns. They chose to pray and worship in a difficult situation, after getting into trouble for doing something good. As they worshipped there was a great earthquake so that even the prison foundation was shaken and immediately all the doors were opened and the chains of all the prisoners were loosed. The jailer awoke from sleep and was about to kill himself, afraid of the repercussions of all his prisoners suddenly set free from their chains, but instead he found salvation and his whole family was saved.

Prayer and worship from the heart shook the place of darkness! God's presence pervaded that prison and good came out of a bad situation. The Lord has a way of turning things around even when sometimes we don't see it straight away.

Jesus Himself was very aware of the power of atmospheres such as in the story where He healed Jairus's daughter (Mark 5:21-41). Jesus was called to the home of Jairus whose daughter was seriously ill, however, by the time He reached the house the little girl was dead and the house was full of weeping and wailing as the mourners gathered. Jesus' response was to send away the people, and taking only Jairus and his wife, Peter, James and John, He went in to the little girl and took her by the hand – immediately she was healed and got up. The atmosphere of death and grief was changed by the presence of Jesus. Instead of death life came into the situation, but it is interesting that Jesus told the mourners and those proclaiming death and hopelessness to leave the situation before He brought life to the little girl.

Acts 9 tells of a similar situation when Peter was called to the deathbed of Tabitha (or Dorcas, which was her Greek name), a lady who had died and whose friends were weeping and crying at her bedside, hoping for a miracle yet grieving and mourning their loss. Peter told all the mourners to leave the room while he prayed for Dorcas and told her, *"Tabitha, get up"*. She opened her eyes and seeing Peter, sat up as she was raised to life.

An environment of grief and mourning is no atmosphere in which to pray for healing and miracles.

Repentance or Revolution

Preaching the gospel, proclaiming His wonderful message and living the life of Jesus causes a shift in the atmosphere around us.

In the eighteenth century the great evangelists John Wesley and George Whitefield travelled many thousands of miles on horseback in Britain preaching and proclaiming the Good News of Jesus Christ. Their preaching was about a real revival of faith and repentance with tens of thousands of new believers. Their preaching touched all levels of society and every part of the country changing the spiritual climate of the nation.

In France, however, around the same time there was the French Revolution. There was social upheaval and great bloodshed and while the cry of the revolution was "Liberty, Equality and Fraternity," for many people it meant death. The atmosphere in the two nations at that time could not have been more different.

Today, atmospheres are still being changed for good. Sometimes it is being done through prayer and proclamation and prophetic voices or the public reading of the Bible as God's word; other times it is though acts of forgiveness, repentance or practical down to earth acts of kindness. I notice when I go now to the Rhondda Valley where I lived for many years, there is a lighter spirit and real ease and a warmth to the things of God. It used to be that people visiting the area would say it was quite a depressing valley to be in, people do not say that anymore. But over the years a lot of prayer, worship and preaching of the Gospel has taken place and we are starting to see the results of this.

Buddhist Convention

In the early years of my ministry I would sometimes work as a nurse to help finance myself. One time, I was asked to care for a very ill gentleman in the Rhondda Valley in the family home. This gentleman loved the Lord Jesus and I remember him requesting for the Bible to be read to him in the Welsh language. His wife would take the Bible and read it out loud to him, it was very beautiful and touching. One of his sons was a practising Buddhist. I noticed that from time to time this Buddhist young man would go into meditations. On one visit I heard that he had just come back from America so I said to him, "How did you get on in America? What did you do there?" He said, "I went to a Buddhist convention in California, 3000 people attended and the first thing we did each morning was *we all meditated and it changed the atmosphere."* I thought to myself, "Yes, I'm sure it did!"

As the worship of idols (false gods), contaminates the atmosphere, so the incredible, awesome, name of Jesus Christ of Nazareth brings cleansing and freedom in the spirit. As this dear mother and father lifted the name of Jesus Christ in their home, no Buddhist spirit was allowed to operate.

If your church does not affect the spiritual atmosphere of your town or city, then the town and city will affect the spiritual atmosphere of your church.

David Holdaway

Changing the Spiritual Atmosphere

3

Building Breakthrough

I noted something very interesting when I visited a church in the north of Scotland with some members of my team a number of years ago. My good friends David and Jan Holdaway were pastors of a church which had gone through great difficulties before they took over ministering there. The church was now doing really well and David and Jan were seeing it grow with people being saved, however, David had asked us to come and pray in the church as on occasions there was a heavy atmosphere present in the church building. He asked if we would join him and Jan and some of the church leaders in praying over and through the building.

I thank the Lord that I had a great team of prayer warriors who had travelled with me from Wales in a minibus for this mission. So we spent part of the week during the daytime praying over the building. We prayed and spoke God's blessing inside the building, we walked and prayed outside the building. An alleyway ran beneath the church which was used as part of the red light district of the city and we went down there and proclaimed God's blessing and cleansing over the entire area. We lifted up the name of the Lord Jesus Christ everywhere; we humbled ourselves before the Lord and repented over any past sins connected with the previous situation and took communion together and read out scriptures aloud.

Some of my favourite scriptures that we read out loud when we are praying cleansing over areas is Colossians 1:13-18,

> *"For he has rescued us from the dominion of darkness and brought us into the kingdom of the Son he loves, in whom we have redemption, the forgiveness of sins. The Son is the image of the invisible God, the firstborn over all creation. For in him all things were created: things in heaven and on earth, visible and invisible, whether thrones or powers or rulers or authorities; all things have been created through him and for him. He is before all things, and in him all things hold together. And he is the head of the body, the church; he is the beginning and the firstborn from among the dead, so that in everything he might have the supremacy."*

And Colossians 2:13-15,

> *"When you were dead in your sins and in the uncircumcision of your flesh, God made you alive with Christ. He forgave us all our sins, having cancelled the charge of our legal indebtedness, which stood against us and condemned us; he has taken it away, nailing it to the cross. And having disarmed the powers and authorities, he made a public spectacle of them, triumphing over them by the cross."*

We went around the church through every room blessing the building in Jesus' name, praying over the doors and anointing them with oil. Prior to David and Jan taking over as pastors there had been a difficult situation with sexual immorality in the church over a long period of time; and although none of us were involved in that situation, we called upon God and asked God's forgiveness for what had happened. We lifted up the name of Jesus and proclaimed the power of the blood of Jesus; we proclaimed the Word of God and the power of His Name. We proclaimed everything good and godly that we could in that place! Scriptures such as: Matthew 1:21; Matthew 18:20; Mark 16:17; Matthew 28:18-20; Romans 3:25; Ephesians 1:7; Ephesians 2:13 and Hebrews 9:11-15.

Entry Points

One of the things that I have learnt while declaring God's blessing over buildings and praying in such situations is that people involved in occultic practices target the doors of churches with curses. Doors are entry points in both the physical and spiritual sense.

In this situation we prayed and anointed the doors with oil (oil being a symbol of the Holy Spirit; Hebrews 1:9; Exodus 40:9) praying God's blessing. We also prayed a lot in tongues (Romans 8:26) and had a powerful time of prayer in one part of the church where we felt there was a particular stronghold. We also prayed in the street and the alleyway underneath the church, praying God's blessing and peace there too. A lot of unclean things had happened in the area.

We all felt that we had had a spiritual breakthrough and from that point the church experienced a real spurt in growth. The heaviness in the church building left, something had shifted in the spiritual realm that allowed the presence of God to come in even greater power. In fact over the next few years David and Jan saw the church grow so much they needed to enlarge their downstairs auditorium, open up the closed balcony and even had to hire other buildings on regular occasions to accommodate the people! And there was constant prayer to keep the "atmosphere" clean and filled with the presence of God.

I was interested to note that the previous pastor of the church had been involved in immoral situations for many years (undiscovered) and it had also come to light that there were immoral situations among some of the believers prior to David and Jan taking over. Not only was the previous pastor in this incredibly sad situation but two other pastors in nearby churches of other denominations had also fallen morally with one of them being sent to prison.

What is interesting to note is that the church was situated right in the centre of the thriving red light district of the city with the working girls even standing not far from the church building. By day the area was a respectable, busy, commercial district, but at night it changed quite dramatically. Many girls worked on the streets in that area and even the alleyway underneath the church was sometimes used by some of the girls!

The encouraging thing is that after the mission the church grew significantly and even started an outreach to the prostitutes in the area with a former prostitute, who had been saved and was a part of the church, a key member of the team. The church also started an outreach to the homeless using cellars that opened out onto the alleyway as a night centre. The atmosphere in the church had changed and was starting to spread to the surrounding area with God's love and power touching and changing lives. It had taken prayer and humility but the effects were very real and grew as the church continued in spiritual breakthrough and seeking God.

Our Responsibilities

While atmospheres can have an effect on us we cannot relinquish our responsibilities in guarding our own lives and of course I understand, "but by the grace of God" we all stand. Also, we understand that as men and women of God, we need to be very careful how we live and that we must be accountable to each other, and it is very important for married partners to protect each other. We know that marriage is a great blessing from God and whilst I believe in a strong moral conduct and to surround ourselves with people of God who are really walking with the Lord and not be in the wrong place at the wrong time, I do think we are most foolish to underestimate the powers of darkness and how they can affect us in our weakness.

A constant prayer we should have is, *"Lord, help us to keep holy, hungry and humble before you with hearts on fire for you,"* (Jude 24; Hebrews 7:25).

We need to realise as well that when sin has been committed it can be an open doorway for the enemy to come and take control of a place. If through sinfulness he has taken advantage and gained a legal access to a place then to regain control we need to pray and repent and declare God's holiness and rule in that place.

I am convinced that atmospheres can change us for good or bad if we are not careful, and that we are in a spiritual battle. It is very important that we do not neglect our personal life of prayer and obviously we need to be accountable to those we love and those around us because we know that anybody can make a mistake. I heard someone say one day that our weakest point is when we think we are so, so strong in a particular area that we could not possibly fall, that is the point where we are the most vulnerable.

Changing the Spiritual Atmosphere

On one occasion I was leading a prayer meeting late on in the evening, and when we had just got into prayer I suddenly had some unclean thoughts come into my head. I realised as I looked around that we were standing in a closed gym and the man who had previously rented the building I knew to be a violent, unclean man. I believe that I was picking up the atmosphere that had been brought into the building by that man, so I bound the unclean spirit and finished the prayer meeting with a song of thanksgiving. It was late and so left the cleansing of the building for another day but by taking authority over the situation the atmosphere no longer affected me.

*Prayer is not overcoming God's reluctance
but laying hold of His willingness.*

Martin Luther

Changing the Spiritual Atmosphere

4

Breakthrough Prayer

It is such a wonderful gift from God that we can meet the Lord at the place of prayer. It is an extraordinary pleasure and strength to know that God is our fortress and we can trust in Him, *"I will say of the Lord, 'he is my refuge and my fortress; my God, in him I will trust,'"* (Psalm 91:2).

I often wonder how people manage through life's circumstances without prayer. Prayer is communicating with the Lord and coming into His presence. I have been very blessed over the years to be supported by many people who pray for me on a regular basis.

I am deeply indebted to the many who have taken time to uphold me before the Lord which has really strengthened me and helped me to stand throughout the years and to minister in all sorts of situations. And over the years there are many things I have learnt about prayer.

Prayer Not Only Changes Circumstances, Prayer Changes Us!

As oxygen is a lifeline for our physical bodies, prayer is a Christian's lifeline to our Almighty God. The Holy Spirit moves us to pray and we can come before Him just as we are.

"Rejoice in the Lord always, again I will say rejoice! Let your gentleness be known to all men. The Lord is at hand. Be anxious for nothing, but in everything by prayer and supplication with thanksgiving, let your requests be made known to God; and the peace of God, which surpasses all understanding, will guard your hearts and minds through Christ Jesus."

Philippians 4:4-7

John Wesley, a great man of God, and the founder of the Methodist movement once said, "It seems God is limited by our prayer life that He can do nothing for humanity unless someone asks Him."

God has chosen to work in response to the prayers of His people. Our Lord Jesus is a wonderful example when it comes to prayer. He did not just tell us to pray, but showed us how to do it. Such was His lifestyle that the disciples never said, "Lord, teach us to preach," rather they asked, *"Lord, teach us to pray"*. Before every important decision in His life, Jesus prayed.

Shutting the Door

I love the scriptures in Matthew 6:6-13 which speak about when we pray we should go into our room and close the door because doors are entrance and exit points; people and things come in through doors and go out through doors.

In the New King James Bible, Matthew 6:6 actually says, *"...pray to your father who is in the secret place."*

I believe that when Jesus speaks about going into your room and shutting the door and your Father in heaven hearing you, He is speaking about shutting the door to doubt, unbelief and distraction – anything that can take your focus away from God – and instead opening the door to faith, belief, hope and expectation.

I love the story in 2 Kings 4:1-7 about the widow and the oil which tells how she went to Elisha, the man of God, because the creditors were coming to take her two sons into slavery as she had debts that she could not pay. Elisha asked the woman what she had in the house. She replied by saying she had nothing except a small portion of oil, just enough for her next dinner. He said to her, *"Go round and ask all your neighbours for empty jars. Don't ask for just a few. Then go inside and shut the door behind you and your sons."* Shutting the door was shutting in faith and belief to believe for a great miracle and shutting out the negative and any criticism that would have stopped her obeying Elisha's words.

Faith – an Important Ingredient

James O. Fraser, who was a missionary with the China Inland Mission, once said, "To pray without faith is like trying to cut something with a blunt knife." When we shut the door, we shut out unbelief, fear, doubt and distractions and everything else that can stop us receiving from God. And instead we shut in faith, thereby believing God for our breakthrough, turning our eyes to our saviour, rather than listening to the negative influences around us.

The place of personal prayer is possibly the most important part of our walk in our Christian life. It is a time of meeting with our Lord, listening to His heart, being open to the Holy Spirit. It is a time when we grow in sensitivity to God's voice and it can be a time of spiritual breakthrough.

The lady in the story was not disappointed as the multiplication of oil happened in front of her and her boys' eyes. God took her from being bankrupt to a business woman in a moment. The fear of what would happen to her family was gone in an instant as God answered her prayer. The atmosphere in that home changed from one of fear and despair to hope, faith and expectancy.

Prayer is Essential

In pioneer evangelism prayer is absolutely essential. *As we pray our hearts are changed* and as we enter into His presence we gain assurance that our prayers are answered as we reach out to Him in faith. The Holy Spirit will guide us as we pray and faith will help us to gain the breakthrough.

The Bible tells us in Psalms that if we cherish iniquity in our heart, God will not hear us (Psalm 66:18), however, as we come to a place of prayer we come first to the assurance of cleansing. *"Do not let the sun go down while you are still angry, and do not give the devil a foothold,"* (Ephesians 4:26). These two scriptures help to keep us on the right track.

The Holy Spirit touches our spirit and cleanses us from the inside out. In Wales we have our own language, the words for Holy Spirit in Welsh are *Ysbryd Glân* which translated means, "clean" or "pure" Spirit. (The verb "to clean" in Welsh is *"glanhau".*) Being cleansed by the Holy Spirit is essential in our walk with God and is the first step to a right relationship with Him.

As we prepare ourselves to enter God's presence we also come with thanksgiving and praise as praise is the language of faith. We can boldly enter into His presence because of the precious blood of Jesus our Saviour. We come led by the Holy Spirit in faith believing and knowing that our Lord hears us.

If we have a personal issue before us and we need to see something shift in the spirit, we need to come before the Lord, call on His mercy and start to pray. We need to pray in English, in tongues and to worship. In my personal prayer time I come and worship, I lift up the name of Jesus and I tell Him I love Him. Then I continue and sometimes I pray for individuals or individual situations and bring them before the Lord.

There is no doubt about it – prayer really changes things. To pray as one individual is good, but if we are going to see an area or a nation changed and a great harvest for the Kingdom, then we need to see the power of collective prayer.

Prayer Walking

One very effective way to pray that I have found over the years is by "prayer walking". It helps you connect with the community and the people who live there and opens our eyes to the needs in that locality. You may have passed the local school, hospital and the homes in an area many times but prayer walking helps you to make a deeper connection with the neighbourhood and have a greater compassion to reach people with the Gospel.

Choose the areas you would like to walk or that you feel God is leading you to and think about what you may like to pray as you walk. You will also find God will reveal specific things or people for you to pray about as you walk and become sensitive to what God is saying about the area.

It's good if you can spilt up into two's or three's rather than going as a large group, but it's also good to keep to a set locality. If you are in a roughish area it's important that ladies and youth do not go alone especially in the evenings. Always be wise in how and where you walk – angels are there to protect us but we also need to be wise to our surroundings. And praise God for mobile phones! Choose a time which suits you, most people go when it's light but some churches go in the evening if people are working and unable to go in the daytime.

Some people like to pray in silence as they walk, others like to pray as if they are having a conversation with the people they are walking with.

Sometimes people like to stop at chosen areas and read the Bible out loud, others pray and with care anoint areas as they go. Be sensitive and follow whatever way you find the Lord is leading you.

When I was a young Christian I was very moved one day when I was standing on the street, a few miles from where I lived, and an older gentleman walked down the other side of the street then stopped, removed his *"dai cap"* and recited two chapters from the book of Corinthians. On finishing he bowed his head and prayed, it was truly beautiful.

Over the years along with a team I have prayer walked a needy area in my city and as we went we called into the shops and businesses we passed and explained who we were and how the Lord Jesus loved them. We asked many of the people if they would like us to pray for God to bless them and no one ever said no. Other times we went into the public houses and asked if we could chat to the customers. We were always received well.

Another time we prepared some letters with the church address and included a tear off slip at the bottom which said that we were praying for the area and if people would like prayer please fill in the slip and we would collect it the next week. The first week we walked and prayed over the area and delivered the letters. On the second week we called to the homes and asked about the letter and offered to pray for people. Many folk asked us into their homes, we prayed for families, for their children, for the elderly. The preparation we had done in prayer walking the area had softened people's hearts and gave us an open door to pray and witness to people.

Expecting From God

We also need to expect from God. Elijah was a man who heard from God and followed His commands. There had been a drought in the land of Israel for three years, yet Elijah heard the rain before it came (...*and Elijah said to Ahab, "Go, eat and drink, for there is the sound of a heavy rain,"* 1 Kings 18:41). I believe if we see or hear something in the spirit we can receive it!

Elijah confronted the prophets of Baal on Mount Carmel and through that encounter evil was defeated – the prophet prayed, the fire fell from heaven and consumed the sacrifice and the prophets of Baal were killed as they were publicly humiliated. Immediately following this event Elijah heard something in the supernatural realm – the sound of heavy rain. While Ahab the king went to eat and drink Elijah the prophet went to pray,

> *"And Elijah went up to the top of Carmel; then he bowed down on the ground, and put his face between his knees, and said to his servant, 'Go up now, look toward the sea.' So he went up and looked, and said, 'There is nothing.' And seven times he said, 'Go again.' Then it came to pass the seventh time that he said,*

'There is a cloud, as small as a man's hand, rising out of the sea!' and after that the rain came and the drought in the land ended."

Elijah heard and expected from God and through prayer it came about. We need to be open to hear and see in the spiritual realm and then pray through to receive what God has for us.

Breaking Through

On one occasion I was ministering with our team in London's East End in a 1,000 seater marquee as part of an evangelistic event.

We were there for two weeks of mission. There were a lot of daytime activities as well as evening celebrations but I felt the evening meetings were very flat. About 600 people came each night which for the location were pretty good numbers. The meetings were nice but I felt no liberty in preaching and I felt it was a really tough spiritual atmosphere. In our ministry we love to organise prayer meetings as part of the day's programme but we could not seem to sense any spiritual victory. It had come to my attention that half a mile down the road was a 2,000 seater Islamic tent and we were surrounded by seventeen abortion clinics.

After the initial few days although we had really prayed it seemed very difficult to break through. I was so glad that we were working with a good local church and I had 30 wonderful team members with me and we were used to praying together. So I said in this one particular prayer meeting, "Come on everybody, let's really call upon the Lord!"

I love what the Bible says in Romans 8:26, *"Likewise the Spirit also helps us in our weaknesses. For we do not know what we should pray for as we ought, but the Spirit Himself makes intercession for us with groanings which cannot be uttered."*

Then we worshipped, danced and praised the Lord. We also took communion together and then prayed and worshipped and prayed and worshipped even more! And sure enough, the Spirit of God came upon us and we went another level into intercession and whatever it was over that tent and over that mission, it broke in Jesus' name!

The following week the meetings went much better. It was easier to minister and there was a better response from the people. I remember one night a man came to receive the Lord as His Saviour and his hand was crippled due to an injury followed by surgery which had not improved the situation. I told the story that night of a little boy I had seen healed in Thailand with a clubbed foot and a lady with crippled feet, how she had also been healed. I remember holding the man's hand in front of me and I was thinking, "This will be a challenge." But I was so pleased I kept my eyes opened because as we prayed in Jesus' name his crippled hand opened and he was healed.

The mission continued and was very successful.

Prophetic Prayer

Paul the apostle called upon the Corinthian Christians to desire spiritual gifts but especially that they may prophesy. We read about this in 1 Corinthians 14:1.

The prophetic voice helps us to pray effectively and can also give confirmation, comfort and sometimes direction when we are seeking the Lord for His will. Two friends and I were just about to travel overnight by car to Scotland from Wales which is a ten hour journey. I had been speaking at a ladies meeting and was just about to leave when an elder in the church walked in and spoke to me. (I had never met him before and he didn't know we were about to make a long journey as we were on our way to conduct a ladies retreat). He said to us, "The situation you are going to will be difficult, but the Lord says to you not to worry because it will have lasting fruit." That was amazingly true and because of the prophetic word we were really encouraged to push through and not give up. Even though we had a difficult and tiring time ahead of us the meetings we were involved in did have lasting fruit, and that word was a great encouragement to us to keep focussed so that God would bless us which He faithfully did!

Prayer, the Prophetic and Proclamation

I have had the joy of doing a number of tent missions over the years with a pastor and his wife from Swansea Valley Bible Church, Andrew and Helen Yeoman. Some of their church had an experience on a mission trip to Poland a few years back and through prayer and prophetic words the team had an amazing breakthrough in a difficult spiritual atmosphere,

> A small group of us travelled to Northern Poland to work in a village alongside a Polish missionary society for young people and students. The intention of the mission trip was to evangelise a small Polish village which, although having a very strong Roman Catholic Church, had never known of the true gospel of Jesus Christ.

We soon found that, despite having a busy evangelistic schedule, including the provision of food, clothes and practical help, we felt powerless and really needed the Lord to come into the situation. We met with the Polish mission team for prayer and cried out to the Lord until late at night for a breakthrough. The following morning we met for prayer again, and it was in this setting that a prophetic word came in which the Lord said that He intended to set up His throne in the village, but that we needed to quicken the pace and be filled with His Spirit. The team was very excited by this.

During the evening meeting the gospel was preached out in the open and almost as soon as the appeal was given, between six and eight teenage girls stood up, all holding hands, and walked towards the front to receive Christ as their Saviour in full view of the whole village.

After the meeting the mission team got together and prayed for those who had been saved that night and those whose lives had been touched – there were many. A policeman who had been at the meeting was heard to say to his partner that he felt the presence of the Lord and thought that as a result of that he should become a priest. He was told by a member of the mission team that this needn't be the case. He simply needed to repent and give his life to Christ. The janitor of the school we were staying around gave her life to Christ in the kitchen with one of the members of the Polish mission team.

As the week went on and we continued to press into what the Lord wanted to do, there came a greater intensity of the Holy Spirit in the atmosphere of the village, and also a greater breakthrough with the people. On the last evening of the mission, around 250 people (out of a village of 800) gathered to hear the Gospel. There was such an immense presence of God in the place that local unbelieving teenagers who were watching and listening to the open air worship began to see visions of the end times. A section of scripture often quoted during the week was Luke 10:1-20. We felt like the seventy being sent out to prepare the way of the Lord.

The prophetic word in this situation made all the difference. The word gave spiritual insight and then the authority to act upon that word through prayer. As a result of this the spiritual atmosphere changed which enabled a breakthrough that affected the community and saw many people saved and touched by God's Spirit.

Africa – Battling Through to Victory

It was a privilege a number of years ago to travel with some of our Harvest Time team consisting of Nigel Phipps, Andrew and Deb Jarvis, Heather Smith, Sarah Trinder, Jenny Grant and Sue King, to Tanzania in East Africa to work alongside John and Debbie Bullock. At the time John was the Regional Director of the Elim work in East Africa. It was a real joy making the journey to that beautiful country visiting churches and also conducting an outdoor evangelistic mission in the north of the country.

The mission was held in the open air in Tanga and about 600 people attended each evening. It was in a strong Muslim area and I'll never forget the rickety platform that we had to stand on – it all seemed rather collapsible! The meeting was very powerful and the worship was extraordinary and the presence of God was clearly felt.

I had the joy of being the preacher that night and was amazed that when I gave the Gospel appeal no one responded. I had thought that in African missions the response would be greater than back home in the UK. I remember it being very hot and humid and we ladies had been advised before we left the UK to wear long sleeve tops and trousers because of the mosquitos. However, the following day we were told that it was not the custom to see godly women in trousers! So I came away not knowing whether the lack of response was because of the trousers or something else in the atmosphere! I have learnt over the years that while prayer and faith are so important we also have to be aware of the culture and customs of the places we minister in.

We were staying in a guest house and some of the team were doubling up in rooms. I was blessed to have my own room. In the morning, two of the team who had shared a room, Sarah Trinder and Heather Smith, mighty women of God, came out of their room in the morning both looking very dishevelled and exhausted which was very unlike them because they always looked very glamorous.

They told us that throughout the night there had been a strong demonic presence in the room and one of them had had the experience of feeling that they were being strangled. They prayed and battled in prayer with this demonic presence throughout the night, hence their dishevelled look. At the breakfast table, as the girls shared their vivid experience John remarked that on the previous occasion that they stayed in that guest house, two of the team had shared that same room and they too had experienced a demonic presence and had spent all night in battle in Jesus' name.

I would not say that we were discouraged at the lack of response the night before but it was of some concern to us, and as in every ministry opportunity, you want to do your best and you want to win many people for Jesus Christ and see a spiritual breakthrough. Nigel Phipps, the Director of our Harvest Time School of Evangelism, suggested we all pray and fast that day believing God for a mighty breakthrough.

He also suggested that we hold the prayer meeting in the same room where the demonic interference was, which we did. We all got down on our knees and prayed and fasted with many tears and cried to God on behalf of the people. Suddenly, as the crescendo of prayer lifted and the power of God fell upon us, we were very conscious that the demonic element in the room had gone and there was a definite shift in the atmosphere. I remember John remarking, "Today I witnessed a change in spiritual atmosphere, an evil presence left the room."

Needless to say, from that time onwards there was a response each evening, with people being saved and healed and we had a report later that many had been saved and added to the church.

I realised that through prayer and fasting, especially as a group when you're united together as one, anything can happen.

C.H. Spurgeon said, "When a man's heart is so stirred that he weeps over the sins of others, he is elect to usefulness. Winners of souls are first weepers for souls as there is no birth without travail, so there is no spiritual harvest without painful tillage. When our own heart is broken with grief at man's transgression, we should break other men's hearts. Tears of earnestness beget tears of repentance. Deep calleth unto deep."

For we do not wrestle against flesh and blood, but against principalities, against powers, against the rulers of the darkness of this age, against spiritual hosts of wickedness in the heavenly places.

Ephesians 6:12

Changing the Spiritual Atmosphere

5

Clash of the Kingdoms

Some years ago I was invited to conduct a mission in the north of England. The church was led by an experienced pastor who worked extremely hard and was very anointed. However, they could not seem to see the church grow to more than thirty people and so I was invited to go and conduct an evangelistic mission with the church to help it to grow.

Prior to the mission a young team from our ministry went to the church to train the church in preparation for the evangelistic outreach. They came home rejoicing! They had had a great time and all had gone well, but on their return the pastor telephoned me and told me about an incident whereby just before the team arrived he went to the church building and outside the main door was a dead bird with its head torn off and its entrails out.

He said to me, "Is there any relevance in this? Because eight years ago, when I came to take the church over, I went to the church one day and there was a dead bird there with its head off and its entrails out by one of the church doors."

He then mentioned to me that the three previous pastors had all fallen in sexual sin. I told him that yes, this was of relevance. At that time we were helping a young woman who had come out of

Satanism and she had mentioned to me that when witches put curses on churches they sometimes killed a bird, drank the blood and hid the dead bird by the entrance of the church and put a curse on the church so that people would not attend. Talking to this young woman helped to give me insight into how those involved in the occult seek to affect and bring heaviness upon churches and those involved in Christian work and how demonic powers, if not recognised and dealt with in Jesus' name, can be so destructive in people's lives and ministries.

I thank the Lord that in the almighty name of Jesus Christ, our awesome wonderful saviour, His name, the power of the blood, His sacrifice on the cross, is above every false and evil practice. We went and had the mission in that church and during the day times we spent a lot of time in prayer and the effect of that demonic curse was well and truly broken. The church outgrew the building it was in and is still a flourishing church today.

We certainly do not need to fear these situations, but neither can we be like ostriches, hiding our heads in the sand being ignorant of the situation. We do not fight flesh and blood but principalities and powers, in Jesus Christ, however, we are more than a match for the devil (Ephesians: 6:10-18)!

Taking Authority

On another occasion on the outskirts of Birmingham, again in our 500 seater marquee, we were facing problems of lawlessness amongst the young people who attended. In fact, as we were setting up the tent the police were visiting the area and taking a woman away in a police car and she was not going quietly! No matter how we tried the children were manic and badly behaved, so again we came to prayer and took hold of the Lord and bound up the spirit of lawlessness in the area and walked around declaring the goodness of our saviour the Lord Jesus. From that point onwards we never had any more disturbances during that mission.

The High Places

In the early years, as I held my first missions in our 500 seater marquee in the Rhondda Valleys bringing together teams of dedicated evangelists on mission, we would pitch the marquee in a central spot and then go up the local mountainsides to the high places where we could overlook the villages. There we would praise and worship Jesus, read the Bible, and then we would take Holy Communion. As we did this, on the mountaintops high above the valleys, we would speak the blessing of God on the villages and the people below and pray to break the power of all curses that had come against the people and the areas.

We had learnt that those involved in the occult would often use the high points of areas to make sacrifices and to curse people and the land. We wanted to break the power of those curses and their negative influence and see the power and kingdom of God come in these places instead.

Following this, we would go to the tent site, praise and worship the Lord and take Holy Communion in the field. I often found this was incredibly powerful as many of our fields have had bad practices and unclean things happen on them. Many times we do not know what may have happened in a place, but God can give insight which helps with our prayer. Prophetic gifting can also be powerful in prayer and intercession in these situations.

I believe that land can be contaminated spiritually and this can hinder the presence and power of God in a place. In the Bible there are four main reasons for the land being defiled:

- Sexual immorality – Leviticus 18:24-30
- Shedding of blood – Numbers 35:33; Ezekiel 9: 9
- Idolatry – Exodus 34:12-16
- Broken Covenants – 2 Samuel 21:1-2

Sometimes it will be clear through local knowledge what has happened in a particular place, other times God will give a revelation. We do not need to know all the details, however, we just need to pray in faith and sensitivity to the Holy Spirit.

On another occasion, we were reaching out to a local community and this time we hired a hall. The first night the place was full and we had lots of young people in attendance, but it was absolute bedlam and I left that night a bit disheartened. So the next day we arrived at the venue a lot earlier; we prayed, worshipped and took Holy Communion together and bound the spirit of witchcraft and declared the wonderful blessings of God upon the hall and especially upon the people who would come along. Well, what a different night we had. The venue was full again but the peace of God was there and there were no disturbances. That night many people responded to the gospel message and were touched by the Lord.

In these instances I am not talking about meetings full of Christians but gatherings full of unsaved people which gives a completely different feel. As we take authority over those powers that seek to intimidate, destroy and cause chaos, we will see the power, the peace and the presence of God fill these places.

The Word of God changes the spiritual atmosphere

Changing the Spiritual Atmosphere

6

Proclaiming the Gospel

I believe there comes a point in prayer when you gain ground in the spirit so that you don't so much pray over certain issues, but you actually *call them into being.*

The power of the tongue is incredibly important and I personally believe that the words we speak definitely change spiritual atmospheres for good or bad. In the book of Genesis, it says, *"God said..."* and the whole of the universe came into being.

I believe words have creative ability, even to the point that the words we speak today help to create our tomorrows. In Proverbs 18:21 it says that *"life and death is in the power of the tongue."*

There is great power in the words we speak. How many times have we met broken people or people battling rejection or who have a rebellious lifestyle because at a crucial time in their lives someone spoke unhealthy words over them? This can be the case particularly when an authority figure, such as a father or a mother, says those words. For example, a mother speaking over her child that they will never be a good parent and will never amount to anything can bring so many negative feelings into that child's life for years to come. However, just as bad words can bring a curse, good words can bring a real blessing.

Good words to speak over our lives and over those of our loved ones are those such as the priestly blessing spoken in Numbers 6:22-27,

> *The LORD bless you and keep you;*
> *The LORD make His face shine upon you,*
> *And be gracious to you;*
> *The LORD lift up His countenance upon you,*
> *And give you peace.*

And the power of words is shown Matthew 8:8, where the Roman Centurion asks Jesus to heal his servant and says, *"Just say the word and my servant will be healed"*.

The Word of God Changes Spiritual Atmospheres

Many years ago, I attended the World Pentecostal Conference held in Oslo, Norway. It was a great time of inspiration and encouragement. In addition to the large conference there were also various daytime activities. For one of them a small tent was set up in the centre of Oslo where they had the public reading of the Word of God over the PA system.

People were invited to read the Word of God publicly in their own language. I had the joy of reading two or three chapters in English over the PA system. The organisers of this great event had tapped into the revelation of the power of the public reading of the Word of God. It didn't matter that it was read in a language that only the reader understood. Whether it was Russian, Spanish, French, Norwegian, Welsh, English or some other language, the fact that it had been spoken over the airwaves into the spiritual realm was what was important.

When we read the Word of God it changes the atmosphere of our heart, (Isaiah 55:10-11).

In the eighteenth century John Wesley, the founder of the Methodist movement, travelled more than 250,000 miles throughout Britain. Wesley publicly proclaimed the Word of God in the open air, in the fields, on the hilltops and throughout towns and villages, and it changed the spiritual atmosphere in many places throughout the land. Wesley's famous experience on May 24, 1738, at a Moravian meeting in Aldersgate Street, London, in which he heard the reading of Martin Luther's preface to the Epistle to the Romans, and penned the now famous line, "I felt my heart strangely warmed," completely revolutionised the character and the method of his ministry (*The Genesis of Methodism*). He preached two or three times a day and Stephen Tomkins writes in his biography of Wesley's life that he rode thousands of miles, gave away £30,000 and preached more than 40,000 sermons. He started a movement that changed the atmosphere of a nation. As I mentioned earlier, while the Methodist Revival took place in our country around the same time the French Revolution took place across the English Channel. Thank God that John Wesley and people like him, such as George Whitefield, did not shrink back from the public proclamation of the Bible and revolutionised Britain in a spiritual way.

Words really do change the atmosphere.

In some countries in the world, even in some cities of the UK, we have Islamic prayers and singing ringing out in Arabic from the minarets, proclaiming the message of Islam. It does not matter if the people don't understand it, it is still influencing the spiritual atmosphere.

Jesus said, *"Go into all the world and preach the gospel,"* (Mark 16:15; Matthew 28:18-20).

The Power of Words

Jesus said that it's not what goes into your mouth that makes you unclean but what comes out of it, (Mark 7:15). We know He reprimanded the religious Pharisees of the day, He said they were like *"whitewashed tombs, which look beautiful on the outside but on the inside are full of the bones of the dead and everything unclean..."* (Matthew 23:27). They had religion and rituals but no real spiritual power.

There is an incident in the Book of Acts when the seven sons of Sceva, a Jewish chief priest, tried to cast an evil spirit out from an individual. However, the evil spirit in the person turned on them and they ran away in defeat. What they did not realise was that it was not just using the name of Jesus that brought freedom, but like Paul, knowing the power of the name of Jesus and having a personal, living relationship with Him that enabled him to have authority in the spiritual realm, (Acts 19:11-17).

I was ministering in a meeting one day and a lady asked for prayer and she said to me, "I'm going to be just like my mother, crippled up with arthritis and in a wheelchair." I said to the lady, "Don't say that," because I realised she was speaking a curse over her life with the words she was saying over herself.

Another day I met a young man who had had several nervous breakdowns. He had come from a very broken situation and said to me that when he was in his late teenage years, he had spoken over himself that he was going to have a nervous breakdown, and sadly that is exactly what happened.

Over the years I have come across many examples of people who have suffered as a result of speaking destructive and negative words over their lives. Thankfully, there is great blessing and fulfilment in praying and proclaiming the scriptures. Use different ones that are close to your heart or that God has spoken to you about. It's good to speak them out loud and to take hold of them and to stand on them. For example: Psalm 1; Psalm 112; 1 Chronicles 4:10. We don't do this as a ritual but because we have faith in the power of God and in His word.

Acts of Kindness

When we have a passion for the Lord Jesus alongside that we should always have a compassion for people, and it is so important that the church should be involved in acts of kindness. Acts of kindness really can change a spiritual atmosphere; kindness is one of the fruit of the Holy Spirit (Galatians 5:22).

However, I don't just want to feed people without telling them of the love of God. What William Booth, the founder of the Salvation Army, said in the East End of London is very true, "You can't preach the gospel to men with empty stomachs."

Acts of kindness and preaching the Gospel are two things that go hand in hand. Sadly, however, I see a trend developing in the UK where we are very involved in social issues, but we sometimes neglect to tell the story of Jesus and share our faith and hope and *why* we are doing these deeds. I am personally involved in acts of kindness in the communities I visit to evangelise, but if we only feed the poor, give a bed to the homeless, give an encouraging word to another but fail in a loving, compassionate, humble way to also tell the message of Jesus we are robbing the people of the greatest treasure ever – forgiveness of sins, eternal life and to know the saviour and a life of His blessing.

There is a heaven to look forward to and a hell to turn away from and surely in the church today, the main message must not be forgotten. *"Life and death is in the power of the tongue,"* Proverbs 18:21.

Geographical Atmospheres

Whilst conducting a mission in the small mining village of Gilfach Goch I realised that the village was mainly in the Rhondda Cynon Taf borough, but the village also bordered on the next borough of Bridgend, an area sad to say, well known for suicides among young people. I was not aware of this until I travelled around the perimeter of this small area and I noticed some artificial flowers placed in a particular spot following the loss of one life. The church leader said to me, "This is where people come to take their lives."

I was amazed to think that people who were living in the Rhondda Cynon Taf locality actually went over the borough boundary (that they didn't even know about), into the Bridgend area and it was there that they committed suicide. I thought, my goodness, it's almost as though a spirit of death or suicide is calling these people. I've noticed that sometimes you find this in open areas, in regions of rivers or bridges, they can become a focal point of spiritual unrest.

Some time ago we were asked to go to look at a needy Welsh valley were there had been three suicides in quite a short period of time; two people had jumped off a bridge and another had jumped from a viaduct. These incidents of sad loss of life were not connected to each other.

A small group of us went to the area where the deaths had happened and called upon the Lord Jesus to cleanse the area. We anointed the places with oil and poured salt into the river, as a sign of cleansing, and we prayed against all suicide and premature death in the area. In faith we believe that this makes a difference in the spiritual atmosphere as we proclaim Jesus' cleansing, presence and blessing in the area.

On one occasion, I was with a team and we were witnessing and sharing our faith in Switzerland on the border with France. It was amazing, on one side of the street in the town we were in the invitations we gave out were well received and people listened to the sharing of the Gospel. On the other side of the street, however, the people did not want to know. I said to the team I was with, how incredible it was that on one side of the street no one seemed to refuse a leaflet and people were very open to the Gospel, but the other side it was totally the opposite – the spiritual difference was so marked between the two sides of the street.

It seems as well that some people who have a powerful ministry can go to one area and they can have a great breakthrough and see healings, salvations and all manner of amazing things, then go to another area and work harder, pray harder but they don't seem to have any spiritual impact at all. Geographical areas really do make a great difference.

The Power of Consecration

About two hours from where I live there is a wonderful Christian retreat centre called Ffald-y-Brenin. People come from all over the world to this little centre that nestles in a small, isolated valley in West Wales and many people have had their lives changed by visiting it.

The most remarkable thing that people comment on when they visit is the sense of the presence of God. In the book *The Grace Outpouring* which tells the story of how Ffald-y-Brenin came into being, Roy Godwin, the Director, tells of the specific instructions God gave him when he was called to make the retreat centre a "house of prayer." God told him,

> "… I want you to walk across the land, I want you to go into the buildings, and this is how I want you to pray…" And He gave me specific instructions on how and what to pray.
>
> He had said three things. First of all, to pray the name of Jesus into the fabric of every room and into the air, the atmosphere of the room, but call on the blood of Jesus, and press the blood of Jesus into everything in the room. This meant the ceiling, the floor, the walls, the doors, the windows and the furniture. So we had to get a step-ladder so we could reach the ceiling and lay hands on them and figuratively press the blood of Jesus into them.
>
> We then had to walk the land, all thirty acres, and say, 'We call on the blood of Jesus and the name of Jesus. We glorify and lift up and exalt the name of Jesus, and we press the blood of Jesus into the land, so it covers every curse, every sin, every other form of bloodshed that has happened here in the past. Every wounding we cover with the blood of Jesus and we press the blood of Jesus into the land.'

The third thing he said was to pray that things would be straightened in the buildings.

As Roy and the team at Ffald-y-Brenin followed these instructions, the presence of God filled the centre and the testimonies of those that have been there bear witness to what can happen when we are obedient to God's instructions, and when land and buildings are consecrated to Him and His presence fills the atmosphere.

Many times as I travel around I visit churches where as soon as I step into the building it is possible to feel the presence of God. Prayer, consecration, worship – it all brings the presence of God into a place and changes the spiritual atmosphere.

God's Timing

I am convinced that sometimes seeing a spiritual breakthrough is also a matter of timing.

My first mission in a marquee was many years ago in West Wales in the beautiful town of Carmarthen. A pastor had invited me to hold the mission and he arranged the marquee and we were there for two weeks. The company we had hired the tent from had double booked so they gave us a tent with holes in it and the generator broke down each night. I had a super team of young people with me and we worked hard, prayed and fasted, spoke in Welsh and English but during the whole mission we never had more than six people respond to the gospel. Although I know it is worth it for the one I must say I was disappointed. I remember saying that one day I will come back to Carmarthen.

Well, many years passed and about twenty years later I was invited to go back to the area and hold an evangelistic event working with a small church there who had a great heart to win the lost. The difference this time was amazing and we saw many people come to faith. In fact I went back and held a mission for four years running and many people found the Lord as saviour and today there is a thriving work there of people who are doing a wonderful work in the community. I think sometimes we sow and sow and need to leave the ground rest and then go back at a later date. When I returned the second time the ground was prepared, the fruit was ready, the atmosphere was so different – it was time for harvest!

In the glory the impossible becomes possible.

David Holdaway

Changing the Spiritual Atmosphere

7

Open Heavens

As far as I am aware there has never been a Christian revival anywhere in the world that has not been preceded by prayer and evangelism. Prayer and evangelism go hand in hand. When we pray, prayer changes us and it changes the atmosphere around us. When we evangelise, it does the same. Together, they are an explosive combination. Whether we evangelise one to one, or have mass evangelistic programmes, sharing the message of Jesus at work, at home or in a wider circle, definitely changes the spiritual atmosphere, especially of our own heart.

My own nation of Wales has an incredible history of revival and is often referred to as a *"Land of Revivals"*. In the eighteenth and nineteenth centuries, there was revival after revival, some localised and some that touched the whole nation. At the turn of the twentieth century there was much prayer going on pleading with God for Him to move once again in the nation. In 1904 in Newquay, West Wales, a young woman named Florrie Evans stood to her feet and publically confessed, *"Rydw i'n caru Arglwydd Iesu Grist a'i holl galon"* (I love the Lord Jesus with all my heart) after being challenged the previous week by the minister in her chapel about her relationship with God. The Holy Spirit seemed to fall on the meeting, some people even say this was the real beginning of the Welsh Revival.

The fire quickly spread to other young people in the Cardiganshire area. Also, during the spring of 1904, a young Welshman named Evan Roberts was repeatedly awakened at 1am and during this time he met with God in prayer until 5am. Revival broke out in Moriah Chapel at Loughor, near Swansea in October 1904 when Roberts held meetings for the young people of the chapel. Within two weeks the Welsh Revival was national news. The meetings broke with convention and bypassed tradition, often the minister just sat down, under God's power, unable to preach. The revival rapidly spread to many parts of Wales as churches "caught the fire" and the Holy Spirit moved throughout the land in great power. News of dramatic conversions, confession of sins and of communities transformed filled the newspapers, and people came from far and wide to see and experience what was happening in Wales.

In the first nine months of the Revival 100,000 people were converted and added to the churches. Some of the most well-known converts were Rees Howells, the intercessor and founder of the Bible College of Wales, Daniel Williams (affectionately known a "Pastor Dan") and his brother William Jones, who went on to pioneer the Apostolic churches, also Stephen Jeffreys and his brother George who founded the Elim Pentecostal Church. Their international evangelistic and healing campaigns resulted in multiple thousands being saved.

This sovereign move of God in 1904-05 spread to Azusa Street in the US, Norway, India, Korea and Russia to mention just some of the countries impacted. One of the marks of true revival is world mission.

I conducted the funeral service of a wonderful man of God, Pastor David Thomas, who had faithfully served the Lord in the Congregational Church in Bristol for 35 years. His father was saved in the Welsh Revival and David had become a preacher in

Bristol and his brother, wife and family became missionaries to China, where they are still serving today. The legacy of Revival can carry on through the generations.

Breaking Through to Breakthrough

The early evangelists and apostolic leaders knew a great secret; to continue in an area until the breakthrough came.

Today, we tend to have evangelistic missions of just a few days and maybe for a week. Breakthrough missions turn the local church spiritually and encourage the church to evangelise and win people to Jesus, and that is how a church really grows. There are times when you are in the right place at the right time with the right people and the Holy Spirit falls.

I belong to the Elim Pentecostal Church and in the early days of the movement, when the Jeffreys brothers, George and Stephen, and the Elim Evangelistic Band that they worked with went into a new area to evangelise, they would go initially with little money and they would take the smallest hall in the town. They would then preach and minister until the breakthrough came accompanied by signs, wonders and miracles and they would soon end up ministering in the largest auditorium in the city!

Repeatedly George Jeffreys would go with his team to carry out an evangelistic mission and quite early on there would be an amazing healing. In Swansea in 1929 for example, a young man called Glyn Thomas, who had a hunchback and suffered severely from epilepsy, went along to one of the meetings being held by George Jeffreys. After prayer he was amazingly healed, he later recounted how in the meeting he,

> "...felt two hands which could have been none other than the hands of my blessed Saviour, placed on my back, and

there before that great crowd, that which the doctors had failed to do for twenty years, the Lord Jesus Christ did with one touch. The hump instantly disappeared and my bones were placed into their right position. The coat which I was wearing hung in folds upon my back. At the same time God delivered me from the epileptic fits."

Glyn was a newspaper seller in the centre of Swansea and was well-known throughout the city, so when he was miraculously healed the news spread like wildfire drawing crowds to the evangelistic meetings. He went on to study for the ministry and pastored churches abroad and in the UK.

Other remarkable healings were recorded all over Britain as George and his team pressed in with prayer, faith and preaching of the Gospel again and again seeing tens of thousands of people impacted. Many, many people were healed, thousands saved and churches were set up all over the country. There is something special about pressing in for breakthrough in an area.

Some years ago, I had a meeting with Pastor Wynne Lewis, who at the time was the General Superintendent of the Elim Pentecostal churches. He said to me, "Marilyn, have you ever considered prolonging your missions?" Up until then I had not. However, the week after this conversation I held a mission in Sandfields, Port Talbot, in our 500 seater tent and the power of God fell so much, that we decided to go for a second week with great success. That was a prelude to what happened next.

Long Eaton

In 1998 we experienced a great hunger in our hearts (myself and the ministry I lead, Harvest Time). At that time the team consisted of a number of dedicated couples and their children;

78

Nigel and Maria Phipps; Graham and Sarah Trinder; Andrew and Deb Jarvis; Dean and Pam Verrier; Alister and Thelma Ferguson; Luis-Marie Worth; Heather Smith; Pam Dix; Audrey Pavitt; Doreen Hinton and Sue King. We travelled together extensively with our 500 seater marquee, lorry and double decker bus in Wales and also into England taking missions and training in evangelism.

Earlier that year, the Lord had impressed on me to take my team to a country in revival and to do it quickly. This happened as I was returning home after an early morning prayer meeting in Treorchy Elim church in the Rhondda Valleys that I was looking after at the time.

Car Crash

Prior to this, I had been involved in a car accident (I was not driving), in my friend's car which was lent to me. It was totally written off when we could not negotiate a bend on a slip road. We ran over a grass verge and straight over the main road crashing into the barrier at the nearest roundabout and knocking the lamp post down. We were all in a bit of a shock but none of us had serious injuries. I'm so grateful to the Lord that He saved us at that time. Hence I had no car so I travelled home in yet another borrowed car. Someone kindly donated money into our ministry and it was expected that I would use that money to buy myself another car, but I did not feel in my spirit that that was what the money should be used for.

On arriving home and whilst making a cup of tea the Lord spoke to me. He said, "Take your team to a country in revival – swiftly." So I rang the people who were donating the money and asked their permission if the money could be used for that purpose. They were delighted and said, "That was what we thought the money should be used for, but we did not want to say anything because we knew you needed a car!"

So soon afterwards twelve of our Harvest Time team travelled for two weeks to the revival that was happening at the time in Pensacola, Florida, being led by Steve Hill and John Kilpatrick; (Nigel and Maria Phipps, Graham and Sarah Trinder, Debs and Andrew Jarvis, Heather and Graham Smith, Pam Verrier, Luis-Marie Worth, Sue king and myself).

We were greatly inspired and touched by the revival there and also, as we prayed together each day. We stayed in a fabulous American apartment which was also a blessing but more than that – our hearts were very touched and from that time we just had a great hunger to pray for God to move.

Hungry Hearts

On our return to Wales, although most of our team were holding down influential and busy jobs, we would meet to pray each day, whether it was an hour here or there. Something was bubbling in our hearts. Then we took a one night meeting in Merthyr Tydfil, South Wales, and the Holy Spirit fell. When I gave the appeal, everybody in the congregation knelt down and we all cried before the Lord. There that night was my supervising pastor, Denis Philips, who came and said to me at the end of the service, "Something special has happened tonight. The ministry has gone to another level, be careful you do not lose it." So I said to Denis, "After praying all these years, to have it, I certainly do not want to lose it! Please come and speak to us." He graciously came to spend time with us and our leadership team and I remember saying to Denis, "Well, if anything is going to break out, it's going to break out in Long Eaton."

I knew the pastors of the Long Eaton Elim Church just outside Nottingham, Michael and Jill Williams, as we were from the same home church in the Rhondda and have known each other for a long time. So I telephoned Michael and said, "Michael, something is happening, can we meet with you before the tent mission?" Nigel Phipps, director of our School of Evangelism and Sarah Trinder, our worship leader, and myself travelled up by car and met Michael halfway in a motorway service station.

Michael was also hungry for God, there was a real stirring in the heart of the church and they had started to have all night prayer meetings on a Friday night. We all came to a decision that day that we would obey the Holy Spirit and that whatever the Lord would tell us to do, we would do it. We were willing to lay our programmes down and go for it.

Sarah was to lead the worship with the backing of Maria, Pam, our gifted pianist, and the Long Eaton worship team. The day came for us to start the mission.

Another Realm

We had planned to go for one week in the local park in the 500 seater marquee. The advertisements had gone out and the prayer gone up. What a wonderful surprise we had the first night. The tent was packed and there were 200–300 people there that Michael, as the pastor, did not know. We entered into another realm as the power of God fell upon the meeting and Jesus started to heal people.

When the appeal was given Pam played the piano and sang, people ran to the front, got on their knees on our old rugged tent carpet and cried to God to be saved.

Every night of the first week was different. One night we were crying. The next night laughing. At the conclusion of the week the tent came down and Michael asked if we could stay for two more days, so the team returned home to Wales except Sarah and myself. I well remember the kindness of the people in Long Eaton and a family who were on holiday allowed us to stay in their home for the two days.

We got down on our knees and prayed. We thanked Jesus for His goodness and we cried to the Lord and said, "Lord, please will you come by your presence? We really want your presence. We *need* your presence." And the Lord spoke to us and said, "When you ask me to come, I'll always come."

The next two nights, which were held in the church building, were electric. Like the tent, the power of God was falling. One of the evenings, everybody, including one of the local publicans who had come along with his family and who were not saved at the time, was laying prostrate on the floor because the power of God was so strong.

Michael had hinted at us staying but he knew we had a busy programme planned and we left for Wales. I remember saying that there was such a desire in my heart to continue but I wanted to be sure.

At that time we had planned eight weeks of mission in Wales. We were going to take a team of 100 people and we had already spent thousands of pounds hiring accommodation for the team. We were going to work with a wonderful woman of God, Pastor Pauline Edwards from North Wales. When I came home I prayed and said, "Lord, I want to do your will. I'm happy to cancel all the programmes, but if we are to go back to Long Eaton then Michael needs to ask me properly as I need to be sure."

You Don't Have Because You Don't Ask!

The next day, Michael phoned me. He said, "We've continued the meetings; they are still powerful but we miss the evangelistic edge. I was praying to the Lord today and He said to me, *'you don't have because you don't ask.'*" I said to him, "We'd love to come, I just need to clear it with the team," and we prayed together over the phone. So Michael and his church leaders prayed, Harvest Time team and myself prayed. We decided we would cancel our planned programme of missions and I explained to Michael that if I came I needed to bring 70 people with me. The church in Long Eaton was incredibly hospitable and for the next six weeks they put up 70 people every week.

What a wonderful time we had! The mission lasted for sixteen weeks. Literally thousands of people came. Our tent was packed every night with people sometimes standing as it was so full. I remember we would have our prayer meetings in the upstairs of our double decker bus, perhaps not the wisest thing to do as there was a lot of us and the praying was very fervent and the bus did sway! Before the meetings we watched the cars and people roll in. Every night people would run to the altar. Healings would occur. Deep repentance. People's lives were touched and changed and healings took place. More than 1600 people responded to the gospel in the sixteen week period.

We had prayed and sought God, as had the church, and the atmosphere in which we were ministering was different to anything we had ever experienced before. The presence and power of God was real and life changing. At the end of the day it is the grace of God, but hunger, prayer, persistence and humbling ourselves before God had opened the door to something wonderful.

I was yet to learn another lesson in the changing of spiritual atmosphere.

*The presence of God is the atmosphere
of the miraculous.*

Marilyn Harry

Changing the Spiritual Atmosphere

8

Not Just Another Meeting

Doreen Hinton, a retired school teacher and wonderful personal evangelist and member of the Harvest Time team, was in Long Eaton for the whole period that the mission took place and attended all of the meetings. She made a handwritten record of what happened in all the services. Here is a taster of what it was like on just one evening in the tent.

Friday August 17, 1998

'Good evening,' Sarah Trinder gives a welcome and we begin singing: *My Lips Shall Praise You, Almighty Saviour* and then *Who Paints the Skies into Glorious Light? Only the Splendour of Jesus.*

Sarah shouts: 'The River is flowing, don't stand on the edge. Jump in!'

There is a huge cheer. We sing it and we cheer over and over again.

(I just cannot keep writing this – I have to lift my hands.)

Sarah says: 'I want to tell you, we are not worshipping a God that is not real. We are worshipping the King of Kings, King

Jesus! Lord – we worship you. Sometimes your mouth cannot shut up. Do you know what it is? It is the Spirit of Jesus. We are going to worship you Jesus. You cleanse our hearts in the *River of Life.*'

(Who else but Sarah would say this?)

'Do you know it is impossible to praise quietly? The Bible says *"Shout to the Lord!"* We are giving a shout to the Lord. It is wonderful. What days we are living in? Like the hymn says: *These are the days of Elijah...of Ezekiel...of Moses. Behold He comes*!'

There is cheering, there is clapping.

Sarah says: 'It is the Year of Jubilee. Yes Lord!'

Next we sing: *My Jesus, My Saviour – Lord, There Is None Like You.* There is such wonderful singing – and speaking in tongues.

Now another hymn:

> *Draw Me Close To You*
> *Never Let Me Go,*
> *You're all I want,*
> *You're all I've ever needed.*
>
> *And I love you, I adore you,*
> *What more can I say,*
> *You cause my love to grow stronger,*
> *With every passing day.*

Pastor Michael Williams: 'Friends, we do not want God for what He can do, we want Him for who His is; lovely, beautiful, terrific, marvellous. Lord – we love you – we honour and adore you. We love you.'

We begin singing again: *Lord We Love You and Adore You.*

There is sweet singing in the Holy Spirit and again: *'Lord Jesus we love you – Jesus – we love you.'*

Sarah: 'Let us listen as this is sung to us. Make it your prayer.

> *You are all I want,*
> *You're all I've ever needed.*
> *You are my desire,*
> *No-one else will do.*
> *'Cause nothing else could take your place,*
> *To feel the warmth of your embrace,*
> *To bring me back to you.*

'The lovely prayer: Lord – You are rising higher and higher and we are desiring you more and more. Lord – You are more costly than silver. Lord – You are more beautiful than gold. Lord we are so grateful that you visit us in these days. We are so thankful – that many come in with pain and sickness. They have gone out without pain and sickness. Thank you for saints who come in encouraged. They are going out commissioned. This is not just another night, a divine purpose will be fulfilled by Your Mighty Hand.

Sarah (so excited): 'Friends – He's here! He's here! Let us enjoy these moments in His presence.'

Now a hymn to sing together – an older hymn: *Here Is Love, Vast As the Ocean'*

And again.

Carl (worship leader) sings it solo to us. Wonderful.

We all stand up and sing again. This time it is the verse: *On the Mount of Crucifixion.*

This lovely hymn is sung over and over again – the moving words just touch us. There is clapping and praise – people speaking in tongues. The atmosphere is electric – but the power is the Holy Spirit.

There follows another lovely hymn. How they blend in harmony: *There Is A River That Flows From God Above.*

We sing it again and again, especially the part, *Come to the Waters, There Is a Vast Supply.*

Pastor Michael and Marilyn and Sarah are on the platform now. Their faces are just glowing.

Song: *Come To the Waters*

Sarah says: 'It's not just for a season. It's a river. It's started to flow.'

Sarah is so excited – rejoicing so much in the Holy Spirit. Nigel and Pastor Michael hold her each side but the power is so great. To the floor Sarah goes, not falling by accident, but under the mighty anointing of the Holy Spirit.

What a thrilling, exciting, wonderful time. Folk are jumping – with true joy. There is clapping, praise, tongues. All so loud...with so many praising.

Marilyn gets the blue flag – her face is glowing as she waves it over the people. Hands are lifted up. Marilyn is shouting: 'Come on lift them up!' The other flags are waved. What excitement – the presence of God is here.

Sarah is on her feet again: 'It's coming!' she calls out. 'Don't worry about your swimming costume! Don't worry what you have got on! Don't worry what folk think! This is a new level!'

Sarah goes to the floor again under the anointing of the Holy Spirit. What are we going to do now?

As people go to the front they are asked to stand in rows – there are three rows. Marilyn tells us: 'This is the time of the supernatural and Christianity was born in the supernatural. If you do not like this...We have learnt a great deal in these days. What you are experiencing here tonight is the edge of the precipice of a Holy Ghost revival. It is time to throw down our pre-conceived ideas. I prepared a sermon last night but never preached it. Tonight is another different night – but it does not matter. If you are religious you will not like this – but it does not matter. Sarah, Pastor Michael, Pastor Dean, Nigel and Maria – you need catchers, for we are going to run through the crowds tonight. Father, we ask you in Your Great Love and Your Great Mercy. They went out with a great shout. I want you all to say that – together: *'They went out with a great shout!'*

Many fall on the floor under the mighty power of the Holy Spirit. There is laughing. Carl and Pam are now singing; *Breathe on Me Breath of God, Until My Heart Is Pure.* Just a few are watching from the back – not many spectating – not partaking. Pam is laughing and crying, Carl is laughing and crying, John is laughing and crying – all on the platform.

Maria leads us, speaking in tongues, in Jesus' Name. *(I was at the corner of the platform, writing these notes.)* Maria laid her hands on me. 'Fresh, fresh anointing,' Maria calls. My knees give way, I went to the floor. Many are laughing and praising, 'Fresh strength and power. Please oh Lord.'

Teresa, the cook for the team, is sitting on the floor – just laughing and laughing. Maureen is in her chair – rejoicing – her hands raised. Some are moaning as if in pain. There are very few on their feet except a fringe of observers.

Changing the Spiritual Atmosphere

There is a loud scream: 'Glory! Glory!'

The musicians are sober enough to play gently, Carl begins to sing:

You laid down your life on the altar,
You drank the cup of suffering
When I was still your enemy,
When I was far away,
When I was broken in my sin,
You brought your Spirit upon me
And put a new heart within me.
Pour out your Spirit
Pour out your Spirit
Pour out your Spirit on me.

There is clapping. Again Carl sings: *Pour Out Your Spirit on Me.*

The flags are being waved: *I'll Follow You Forever, You've Always Been My Friend.*

A man beside me, a big heavy man, he just fell back to the ground. No one touched him – just the mighty power of God who is present.

All the musicians play: *Pour Out Your Spirit On Me.*

We sing this over and over again.

Pastor Michael went to see a lovely couple who were at the tent for the first time. The lady had come for healing – and she was healed – walking across the field, not only healed, but that night both of them found the Lord Jesus as their Saviour.

A man on crutches comes out. Susan plays again on the cornet, accompanied by the drums: *My Jesus, My Saviour, Lord, There Is None Like You.*

Marilyn begins: 'We have had a crash course in the past few weeks on how to move in the Holy Ghost. I just knew it was right to run round and wave the flag, and me, my size! God is restoring passion for His church. Jesus is restoring passion for Him in His church. Jesus is looking for Christians who will be sold out for Him! *Passion* – an intense desire that consumes you. The twelve disciples, they had passion. In England, we need a passion for the things of God.'

Marilyn gives examples of Christians with passion: 'William Carey was from a poor family. His father was a weaver and William became an apprentice shoemaker at fourteen. At eighteen he trusted Christ as his Saviour. He became a Baptist Pastor, then a missionary to India. There were hard times with his family, but two passions kept him there and he translated the Bible into Bengali, the language of 300 million people. This passion is emphasised in every revival.

'During the Welsh Revival, 100,000 people came to Christ. The gospel spread – to Azusa Street in the USA, to Norway, to Sunderland, and back to Wales. In the coal mines of Wales, those saved spoke to the horses without swearing and they did not understand. In my village today the long Salvation Army Penitent Bench is in the museum. How upsetting. We have lost the passion for Jesus. God is looking for Christians with passion for Him. In Roman times, many died because of their passion for Jesus. People have passion for sport, for jobs and for different things. Where is my passion for God? Jesus will come back. At His second coming, where do we stand before God? How can this passion be aroused?

'John 3:16 shows the passion of God for you and for me. We will say the verse – out loud, all together – and again. Some go to church but have no passion for God. The church in England needs passion again.

'Luke 23:35 says: *'He saved others, let Him save Himself if He is the Christ of God, the Chosen One'*. How they sneered, but Christ showed His compassion on the cross and still this *passion* is for you and me. Christianity is to be talked about and lived. Think of the woman of Samaria in John 4. When she met the Messiah she went and told the others in her village. It is not just attending church and singing in the choir, nor is it attending a church and being bored. It is about having a passion for Jesus, which means a passion for people.

'God sent His most precious, His Son, and this is the greatest proof of God's love. We see a change in men and women who are forgiven by the Lord Jesus. To become a Christian, to know Jesus, this is the time to come home.

'It is not by giving money to the church or even attending church, nor by doing good that we become Christians. Today, one person in seven claim to know the Lord Jesus as their Saviour. There is a tremendous move of God – not just in Africa and Asia but also in the UK.

'Christians – have you lost your passion?' Marilyn asks. 'This is a time for repentance, humility, and getting serious before God. Will you say "Lord, touch me? Make me passionate?" Passion can be restored. It affects the way that you view other people. If you do not go to a Holy Ghost church, then pray for your Pastor and for your church.

'Thank you, Lord,' Marilyn says, 'to serve you is not boring.'

Pam begins to sing. Many hands are raised and people come to the front. The Holy Spirit is dealing with people. Many are going to the front. Pam continues to sing: *Mercy – For The Nation.*

'Be sure in your heart that there is not any unconfessed sin nor any doubtful habit enslaving you!' Marilyn calls again and still more come from the congregation.

A lovely baby, Katie, who is fostered is brought for prayer. This baby is blind and has severe brain damage. A miracle is needed. Many gather round and Pastor Michael is crying as he prays: 'Lord Jesus, take this lovely child in your arms. Lord Jesus, Son of the Lord God, recreate, restore and renew. Oh God, Oh God, say the Word, Lord Jesus.'

There is praying in tongues and the music plays softly. Prayer continues: 'For John and Sue, the foster parents, Lord encourage them. May these eyes be opened – may the brain be healed.'

'John and Sue have come faithfully from South Wales. We are standing with them,' Marilyn says, 'and we are believing God.'

'We've been seeing tremendous miracles this week,' she continues. 'A heavy man came in on crutches. He talked with me as he came in. Yes, he wanted a touch from the Lord. He received it! As he was prayed for he went to the floor. Did he know Jesus? His answer was yes! Seven months ago he came to Jesus.'

There is music and singing as people are prayed for:

> 'Mercy Is Falling, Is Falling, Is Falling.
> Hey Ho, I Receive Your Mercy'.

Many are dancing and folk are dropping.

Pastor Michael says: 'We bless you, Lord, we exalt you, we magnify your name.'

A man aged 73 comes to tell of a miracle. For 23 years he has known deafness and now he is hearing over the noise of the music.

Marilyn asks him: 'What do you believe? What has Jesus done for you tonight?'

'I can hear you now,' the man says. 'Praise the Lord!'

Pastor Michael: 'We rejoice in God tonight. Let's give God a great hand of praise!'

We indeed do, as everyone claps.

'Glory to God. Have we strength for one more?' He asks, 'Glory to God!'

Carl leads the singing:

> *I Could Sing A Thousand Songs,*
> *How He Saved My Soul.*

Everyone is dancing. Sue Evans plays on the cornet: *Stand Up, Stand Up For Jesus.*

It is time to go – but we want to stay.

Everyone is so happy.

An Open Heaven

We were truly experiencing an open heaven. I have never experienced anything like it. Even the BBC news reported on the meetings as they were having such an impact in the region. After some time the council told us we had to leave the site we were on, we had been there so many weeks, so we moved to a place called *Rosemary's Flower Garden* just outside Long Eaton. It was really tough when we first moved location, some local people gave me the history of the area and explained to me the area had been used as an ammunition factory and all the surrounding area was affected by that work. The Assemblies of God church in Nottingham kindly loaned us their ground to use. The mission continued but with a difference. The atmosphere was hard and we had to really press through. The open heaven we had experienced in Long Eaton was not the same here but we persevered in prayer, worship and after two weeks the fire of God fell again in the meetings.

Holding Christian services each evening with open hearts full of worship and praise really does shift the atmosphere and of course it's *the presence of God that changes things and where God's presence is there will be miracles.*

There is a trend now in the church to believe that proclamation evangelism is not relevant for today. This is an absolute mistake and those like myself who have spent our lives in pioneer proclamation evangelism accompanied by signs, wonders and miracles and mercy ministry, know just how relevant it is in today's twenty first century.

Changing the Spiritual Atmosphere

There was 'life' in the air.

The town of Rhos in the Welsh Revival 1904/05

Changing the Spiritual Atmosphere

9

Opening up the Wells

I had a long standing invitation to hold an evangelistic mission in a church in middle England, the invitation coming from the senior pastor some two years previously. When I arrived, I found that the senior pastor had recently moved to another church and the assistant pastor was now overseeing the work until the appointment of a new pastor. As soon as I arrived the pastor began telling me all the problems of the church. At the time I was tired, this was to be my last mission of the year and I was still recovering from previously being unwell. I did not feel like being there in the circumstances so I asked the pastor, "Are you sure it's right for me to be here? Would you rather I cancel my visit?" In all fairness to him, he said, "Oh no, we have really prayed and believe it is right for you to come," so we went to the first evening meeting.

The church elder convened, he was a man in his middle thirties and after welcoming the people, he handed the meeting over to an older lady and she started to play the piano for a short while. I think she found the songs difficult to play and so gave up and then handed over to the elder who then began to lead worship with his guitar at which point his guitar string broke so he handed the meeting over to me.

Now I must say, I am not able to carry a tune well but I had a go… a very bad go, but the Holy Spirit fell on the meeting and we had a fantastic time.

Lots of people turned up at the meetings and every night there was an incredible move of God. People were saved, healed, baptised in the Holy Spirit and I asked the pastor, "What is the history of this church?" He said to me, "The previous pastor many years ago, had a strong healing anointing and he would arrange for three day healing conventions and the power of God would fall so much, they would turn into three week long meetings." So I knew it was nothing to do with me. I was weak, tired, wanting to go home but I hit oil! I had hit a well of healings and miracles that had been dug over many years by godly people. I was so pleased I never gave up as I had wanted to.

The Outer Hebrides

In 1949 there was a wonderful Christian revival that broke out in the Outer Hebrides, in the north of Scotland. There was an incredible move of God's Holy Spirit where many people received Christ as their saviour and deep conviction of sin came upon the people. The stories are amazing about how even when some of the hardened sailors were aboard ships and they passed certain areas close to the land where the revival was taking place they would get down on their knees and repent and get born again. This revival had been preceded by many people praying and crying out to God.

You've probably heard about the story of the two sisters, Peggy and Chrissie Smith, one was 84 and the other 82 years old. One was blind and the other sister crippled, doubled up with arthritis, and they were praying for revival as not one young person was attending the church at the time. Peggy asked the minister of the church in Barvas, James Murray MacKay, to call the church leaders to prayer. Three nights a week the leaders prayed together for months. One night, having begun to pray at 10pm, a young deacon from the Free Church read Psalm 24 and challenged everyone to be clean before God. As they waited on God His awesome presence swept over them in the barn where they were praying at four o'clock in the morning.

The invitation went out to Rev Duncan Campbell to come to the island from the minister, Rev MacKay, and on the third invitation he responded and went to the Isle of Lewis. Duncan Campbell was the main speaker at a conference when God spoke to him and told him to take up the invitation to go to Barvas. He put his notes in his briefcase and said, "I have to go to the Outer Hebrides." Within ten days he was on the island of Lewis.

At the close of his first meeting in the Presbyterian Church in Barvas the travel weary preacher was invited to join an all-night prayer meeting. Thirty people gathered for prayer in a nearby cottage. Duncan Campbell described it, "God was beginning to move, the heavens were opening, and we were there on our faces before God. Three o'clock in the morning came, and *God swept in*. About a dozen men and women lay prostrate on the floor, speechless. Something had happened; we knew that the forces of darkness were going to be driven back, and men were going to be delivered. We left the cottage at 3am to discover men and women seeking God. I walked along a country road, and found three men on their faces, crying to God for mercy. There was a light in every home, no one seemed to think of sleep."

God had heard the cry of the people and wonderfully brought about a great revival through the prayers that were prayed and through the ministry of Duncan Campbell. In the 2008 documentary film *Great Christian Revivals* Duncan Campbell is quoted describing what it was like to live in a situation where the Spirit of God was moving in such an amazing way, "Revival is a community saturated with God." It was said that seventy-five per cent of the people were gloriously saved before they even came near a meeting...the power of God was moving so much! The spiritual atmosphere on that island had changed and was full of the life changing power of the Holy Spirit!

Living in the Glory

I visited the Isle of Lewis on a holiday with some of my friends a few years ago and was taken to visit some of the people who still remembered the revival. They were all older by then but I asked them what it was like at the time of the revival. They all said the same thing – when the revival broke out, "all we wanted to do was to speak about Jesus." And their faces absolutely shone with the presence of God as they spoke about what had happened.

The pastor at the time of our visit told us the story of a business man who had stood up in the congregation and cried to God and said, "Lord, if you don't answer our prayers now, how will we know we can trust you in the matter ever again?"

One of my friends, Nina Halshall, lived in the Hebrides for a short while some years ago and we visited the home of Nina's friend where Duncan Campbell had stayed and held meetings. Nina's friend was the daughter of the house and had just arrived back from America when the revival was happening. She wondered what was going on and told me that one day, the power of God hit her while she was in the hall of the house and she was wonderfully converted.

Some years ago, Nina was staying in that house in one of the upstairs bedrooms. She came down for tea and said to the lady of the house, "It's been a beautiful day today. The sun has been shining in the bedroom all day."

Nina's friend said, "Oh Nina, it's been raining all day today. But that was the room Duncan Campbell stayed in and the glory of God always comes there."

Northampton and an Angel from Heaven

I was invited to hold a two week mission with a large marquee in Northampton. We were working with a great church and with the Pastor, Gareth Lewis, and everyone had really prepared for the mission which was going very well. We had good attendances each night but I felt that we needed to push for a greater breakthrough. We had experienced some wonderful healings in the healing clinic that we held during the day, including a little girl, three years of age who was malnourished because of a feeding problem.

The meetings were good but we were believing the Lord for a real breakthrough! A Filipino lady pastor, Lily, from London, came and helped us for two weeks. Each lunch time, Lily would come to the apartment I was staying in, which was part of the church complex. We would have a quick cup of tea and then pray solidly for an hour. We would get on our knees and call upon the Lord and ask Him to "disturb" the meetings with His presence. We just wanted to see a breakthrough.

On one of those days as we began to pray suddenly the presence of God filled the room. Lily ran out of the room! (She told me afterwards that she felt God wanted to speak to me.) I looked up and in the doorway there stood a very big figure which completely filled the door frame. I could only see up to his shoulders but he was dressed in a silver gown. Over the silver gown was a robe, also in silver, with two gold braids coming down the front. I presumed it was an angel from the Lord. I had never experienced anything like it before. The presence of God was so awesome all I could do was lie on my face before God and He gave me the words to speak on that night from Isaiah 6.

I stayed on the floor on my face, right up until the time when I got up to go to the evening service. That night it was like all heaven broke loose. We certainly had the breakthrough we had been praying for. The Holy Spirit fell upon the children and the little children who would normally go to the Boomerang Club, the children's work, were lying on the floor with their hands raised to heaven.

The next days were amazing as the Holy Spirit also fell upon the young people and they fell off their chairs under the power of God! Then the Holy Spirit fell upon the older people. Many people were baptised in the Holy Spirit and there was certainly a change in the spiritual atmosphere.

I had never seen silver or gold before like I saw on that angel until more recently when I visited the House of Lords and in the throne area, where our Queen sits for the State Opening of Parliament, the gold in that area looked the same as the gold on the robe of the angelic being standing in the doorway. It was amazing.

God blessed that time so much that the mission went on for six weeks. I was not able to stay for all of that time but that did not matter. The presence of God came in an amazing fashion and God's people were running with it!

Whatever captures our hearts will control our lives and determine our destiny.

David Holdaway

Changing the Spiritual Atmosphere

10

Preparing our Hearts

If we want God to use us in seeing the spiritual atmosphere around us changed, then we have to look at our own lives, to make sure the atmosphere in our hearts, minds and spirits is right before Him.

Communion

If we are going to transform spiritual atmospheres through prayer we need to be in a place of faith and unity with the people we are praying with. Taking communion together is a very powerful sacrament that unifies us as we share together. Jesus said, *"This cup is the new covenant in My blood. This do, as often as you drink it, in remembrance of Me. For as often as you eat this bread and drink this cup, you proclaim the Lord's death till He comes"*, 1 Corinthians 11:25,26.

When we take communion together on mission we are reminded of the sacrifice and victory of the cross and Jesus' great love for us and how He has completely triumphed over every work of darkness. We come with praise and thanksgiving to our Saviour who through His death and resurrection brings us forgiveness and disarmed principalities and powers (Colossians 2:14-15).

Also, it reminds us that Jesus is coming again to rule and reign in power and glory. This gives us grounds of authority to walk in His love and compassion in the unreached areas in front of us (Revelation 12:1). I think that sometimes parks and other outside areas have been used for unclean actions, whether immoral, violent or maybe used in an unholy way with unholy language spoken over them, taking communion reminds us of the cleansing power of the precious blood of Jesus.

Communion symbolizes not only our love for God and His love for us but also our love for each other and it declares God's presence in the place. I have found over the years that taking communion in unity with my brothers and sisters in Christ, opens up the way for God to come into a situation or a place and to move in a wonderful and powerful way.

Unity of Believers

Some of the last prayers that Jesus prayed was for believers to be as one,

> *"I do not pray for these alone, but also for those who will believe in Me through their word; that they all may be one, as You, Father, are in Me, and I in You; that they also may be one in us, that the world may believe that You sent Me. And the glory which You gave Me I have given them, that they may be one just as We are one: I in them, and You in Me; that they may be made perfect in one, and that the*

world may know that You have sent Me, and
have loved them as You have loved Me..."

John 17:20-23

Many years ago, a city wide mission was to be held in Liverpool with Dr Billy Graham, one of the world's greatest evangelists. Prior to this event someone had taken a photograph of Dr Graham talking to the then Pope of the day, as a result a number of church leaders in the city said they would not get involved in the mission.

In view of this George Verwer, founder of Operation Mobilisation, came to speak to the church leaders and approximately 400 leaders attended. I was a young minister at the time and will never forget what George said. He spoke words of praise about Dr Graham and said how he had found Christ as a result of Dr Graham's ministry when he was a young man. Then he said something like this, "We may not agree with everything Dr Graham does, but then I don't agree with everything my wife does! But we are still working together in our marriage." I thought how wise those words were. There are times when we may not agree with everything someone does, but we need to look at what unites us and see how we can work together on common ground for the sake of the Gospel.

Psalm 133 says *"Behold, how good and how pleasant it is for brethren to dwell together in unity!"* In Ephesians 4:3 the Apostle Paul talks about *"endeavouring to keep the unity of the Spirit in the bond of peace"*. I notice that when the Holy Spirit fell on the early believers who were in The Upper Room as recorded in the Book of Acts 2 they were *"all together in one place"*.

One time recently, I was in a needy housing estate outreach meeting and it was so good to see thirty adults and forty children from the estate enjoying a cooked breakfast and having a great time together. It was only able to take place because two churches had faithfully worked together using their different gifts to bless the people. I have noticed over the years that more and more believers are working together with great success to share the wonderful Gospel message.

We really do need each other and we are stronger together than by ourselves. We all have different strengths and weaknesses but that can make us stronger together as we complement each other's ministries.

The task ahead of us is great but together we can do something wonderful in our local communities and further afield. Evangelism can be a catalyst to bring churches together for great purpose. Evangelism can also be an opportunity to lay down our differences for the sake of sharing the Gospel giving many people an opportunity to hear about and accept Jesus Christ as their Saviour. It can affect their eternal destiny!

The Power of Forgiveness

Jesus spoke some amazing words about forgiveness,

> *"Whenever you stand praying, if you have anything against anyone, forgive him that your Father in heaven may also forgive you your trespasses. But if you do not forgive, neither will your father in heaven forgive your trespasses."*

Mark 11:25-26

Rwanda

I have been privileged to visit and minister in Rwanda in central east Africa a number of times. It is a country that has gone through tragic times for many years. During approximately a one hundred day period from April 7, 1994, to mid-July, an estimated 500,000–1,000,000 Rwandans were killed. The *Rwandan Genocide* was a mass slaughter of Tutsi and moderate Hutu by members of the majority Hutu tribe. As much as 20 per cent of the country's total population and 70 per cent of the Tutsi then living in Rwanda were murdered in what is one of the worst genocides in recent decades.

On one visit to Rwanda some of the pastors told me that following the genocide it didn't rain for at least three years and that some areas were so barren due to the drought they were like a desert. I asked them which areas were the ones most affected and they said to me that it was the places where there was the greatest bloodshed. I felt it was reminiscent of the blessings and curses recorded in Deuteronomy 28.

It also reminded me of the scriptures which speak about the blood calling out from the ground, Genesis 4:10, after Cain killed his brother Abel. I believe that acts of violence and the shedding of blood affects the land. We thank the Lord because the opposite is also true – that the precious shed blood of Jesus Christ brings cleansing, even to areas and lands, and it starts in our hearts.

One of the leading pastors in Rwanda told me that as the blood, through violence, had contaminated the land, the preaching of the gospel message of repentance and forgiveness was bringing cleansing to this African soil and bringing hope for a new day.

I've never heard such stories of forgiveness in any nation amongst any people as I have from those dear people who have suffered so much and yet found forgiveness in their heart towards those who had done such great evil. Forgiveness has an incredible power to change spiritual atmospheres as are acts of kindness in opposition to acts of evil.

One couple I know very well suffered the terrible loss of 60 members of their family being brutally murdered in the genocide in that country. But by the grace and mercy of God helping them they have chosen to forgive those responsible for these evil deeds and have even established a nursery school for the children of those who murdered their family.

Forgiveness in Action

Jesus speaks a lot on forgiveness in the Bible. Peter went to Him one day and said, *"Lord, how many times shall I forgive my brother or sister who sins against me? Up to seven times?" Jesus answered, "I tell you, not seven times, but seventy-seven times."* Which is really indicative that we should always forgive.

Jesus also uses the example in Matthew 18:21-35 about the unforgiving servant and the account of the sinful woman in Luke 7:36-50. Jesus said about the woman, *"...her many sins have been forgiven – as her great love has shown. But whoever has been forgiven little loves little."*

The Bible also says that before we take communion we should examine our heart and if we hold anything against our brother, we should go put it right first and then take communion (1 Corinthians 11:23-34).

Jesus spoke about having faith as small as a mustard seed and being able to cast a mountain into the sea. It speaks so much of forgiveness. Jesus is our amazing example of forgiveness. When

He was about to be arrested in the Garden of Gethsemane and Peter took the sword and cut off the ear of Malchus, the High Priest's servant, the Lord rebuked Peter and healed the servant's ear. Some of the last words of Jesus on the cross were words of forgiveness, *"Father forgive them for they know not what they do"*. To think that when Jesus died on the cross and shed His precious blood, it was forgiveness not only in words but also in action. He died for us while we were still sinners (Romans 5:8).

People often ask "who put Jesus on the cross?" and some people say that it was the religious people of the day. They sent Jesus for an unjust trial as they did not have the right to pass the death penalty in Judea at that time and if they had had the right, Jesus' death would have been by stoning. But of course God the Father, in His infinite love and mercy, chose to send His son to the cross, because the Bible says, *"Christ redeemed us from the curse of the law, having become a curse for us; for it is written, cursed is every one that hangs on a tree,"* (Galatians 3:13). What an incredible divine exchange. Jesus, who knew no sin, was made sin for us that we might become the righteousness of God in Him.

When we look at the Bible it tells us that it was not the Roman soldiers or the Jewish priests of the day who crucified Jesus, but the Bible says, in Isaiah 53, that the Father put Him on the cross. Jesus died for our sins that we may be forgiven.

In the course of ministry over the years, I have realised that forgiveness, repentance, renunciation of sin and the forgiveness and release of others is incredibly important in our healing. It is amazing when you pray for an individual who has been bound because of some awful thing that has happened to them, to see them by the grace of God proclaim their forgiveness to the perpetrator. That brings incredible release.

I have been in the ministry long enough to know that except by the grace of God, forgiveness is not always easy as some people have been through some terrible situations. I believe though that forgiveness begins with a decision of our will. It is not a feeling and it does not mean that the person deserves to be forgiven but we need to leave that to the Lord. The important thing is that the pain of what has been done to us can be released through that decision to forgive. Forgiveness brings freedom and changes the atmosphere around us as God's grace and presence can flow in.

I was ministering at a meeting one evening and just at the end, one of the worship leaders came and sat next to me. This lovely young lady was walking with two crutches and as soon as she came and sat by me I had the sense that she had unforgiveness toward her mother. The young woman said to me, "Will you pray for me?" I said, "Yes." And I gently said, "I don't know, but as you came and sat down I just had this thought, that maybe someone had hurt you and you have a problem with forgiving them." The young woman cried out and said, "It is my mother. I can't forgive my mother!" God showed mercy on that young woman that day and she chose to make a decision to forgive her mother even though she did not feel like doing it.

As we know, words are incredibly powerful, so she spoke out loud and prayed a prayer to forgive her mother and then I prayed for her healing. She was not healed immediately, but I met her a few months later and she was totally healed. I felt sure her forgiving her mother played a part in her healing.

There are many ways that we can find freedom and breakthrough in our lives, in our communities and in our families. And breaking through brings with it the life changing presence of Jesus. It changes the atmosphere in which we live and minister. It brings life and healing and wholeness. It can change eternity.

Epilogue

Thank you for taking the time to read this book. I hope you are encouraged and inspired by the truth that people can change atmospheres in the world today for good.

Our God is good. Our loving Heavenly Father is looking out for us, what a treasure it is to know Him, "The great *I am.*"

I believe that changing atmospheres starts with us as we allow the Holy Spirit to touch and change and heal us, to make us whole so that we might be a blessing to others.

Ephesians 2:10 encourages me,

"For we are God's masterpiece, He has created us anew in Christ Jesus, so we can do the good things He planned for us long ago." (New Living Translation)

May we continue to be changers of atmospheres in today's world for good, bringing light where there is darkness, love where there is none, peace in the middle of trouble and hope where none is to be found.

Jesus' words sum it up,

'You must love the LORD your God with all your heart, all your soul, and all your mind.' This is the first and greatest commandment. A second is equally important: 'Love your neighbour as yourself.' Matthew 22:37-39 (New Living Translation).

Changing the Spiritual Atmosphere

Sarah's Song

This book is dedicated to my dear friend, the late Sarah Trinder who is now rejoicing in glory. Sarah had a heart for revival and God's presence like no one I have ever known.

At a *Daughters of Jerusalem* ladies meeting several years ago in Porthcawl, South Wales, Sarah felt God giving her words to a song, a very special song to those of us who live in Wales – our national anthem which is called The Land of My Fathers *(Mae Hen Wlad Fy Nhadau)*. This song is sung in Welsh at all our important national and sporting events. The words God gave to Sarah, however, were about revival – a prayer and a promise for God to once again touch our land of Wales. Here are the words of that song. We sing them at many of our *Love Wales* events. As you sing them pray for God to touch our nation, that the atmosphere of the land will once again be filled with the presence of God!

The land of my Father – the land that you gave.
This land our inheritance, this land shall be saved!
The Good News of Jesus shall flow from these shores.
Revival is coming once more!

Wales! Wales!
We prophesy that you shall be saved!
With one heart and voice, we join hands and rejoice,
That Jesus is Lord over Wales!

Words by Sarah Trinder

119

Changing the Spiritual Atmosphere

Love Wales and Other Resources Available

How To Lead A Person To Christ by Marilyn Harry
An excellent guide on how to witness and share your
faith.

Since 2013 Marilyn has been heading up an
organisation called *Love Wales* with the vision of:

*The re-evangelisation of Wales over the next ten years
by working together across denominations lifting up the
name of Jesus Christ our Saviour.*

If you would like to know more about *Love Wales* and
to support missions and prayer for Revival in Wales
please contact us at:

www.lovewales.org
Email: lovewales@live.com
Tel: 01685 379221